FOO FIGHTERS
WASTING LIGHT

Music transcriptions by Pete Billmann, Addi Booth, Paul Pappas and David Stocker

ISBN 978-1-4584-0800-6

7777 W. BLUEMOUND RD. P.O. BOX 13819 MILWAUKEE, WI 53213

For all works contained herein:
Unauthorized copying, arranging, adapting, recording, Internet posting, public performance,
or other distribution of the printed music in this publication is an infringement of copyright.
Infringers are liable under the law.

Visit Hal Leonard Online at
www.halleonard.com

4	BRIDGE BURNING
15	ROPE
25	DEAR ROSEMARY
36	WHITE LIMO
46	ARLANDRIA
60	THESE DAYS
69	BACK & FORTH
79	A MATTER OF TIME
92	MISS THE MISERY
101	I SHOULD HAVE KNOWN
112	WALK
125	Guitar Notation Legend

Bridge Burning

Words and Music by David Grohl, Taylor Hawkins, Christopher Shiflett, Nate Mendel and Pat Smear

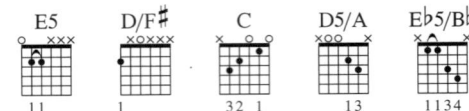

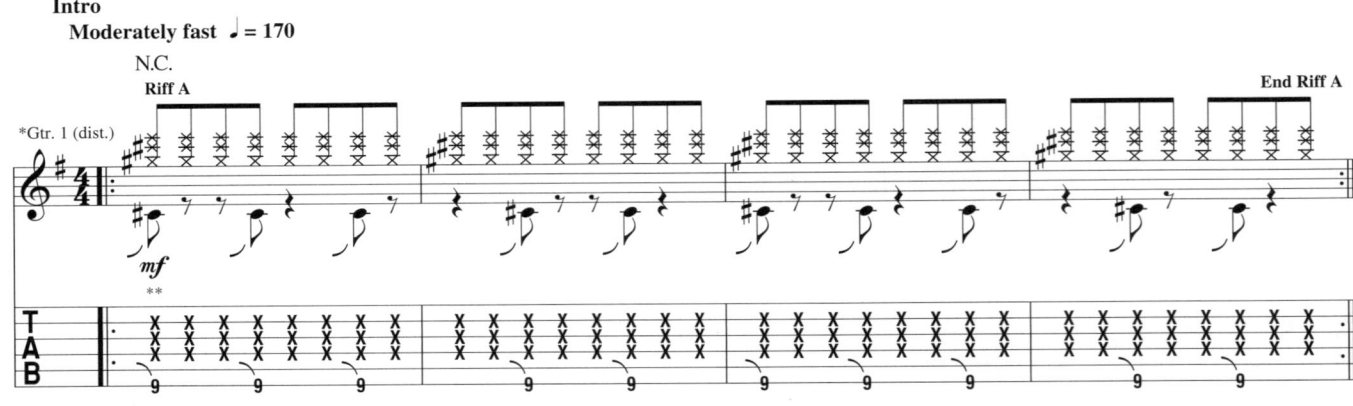

*Two gtrs. arr. for one.
**Hammer on low note w/ left hand while strumming muted notes behind the bridge.

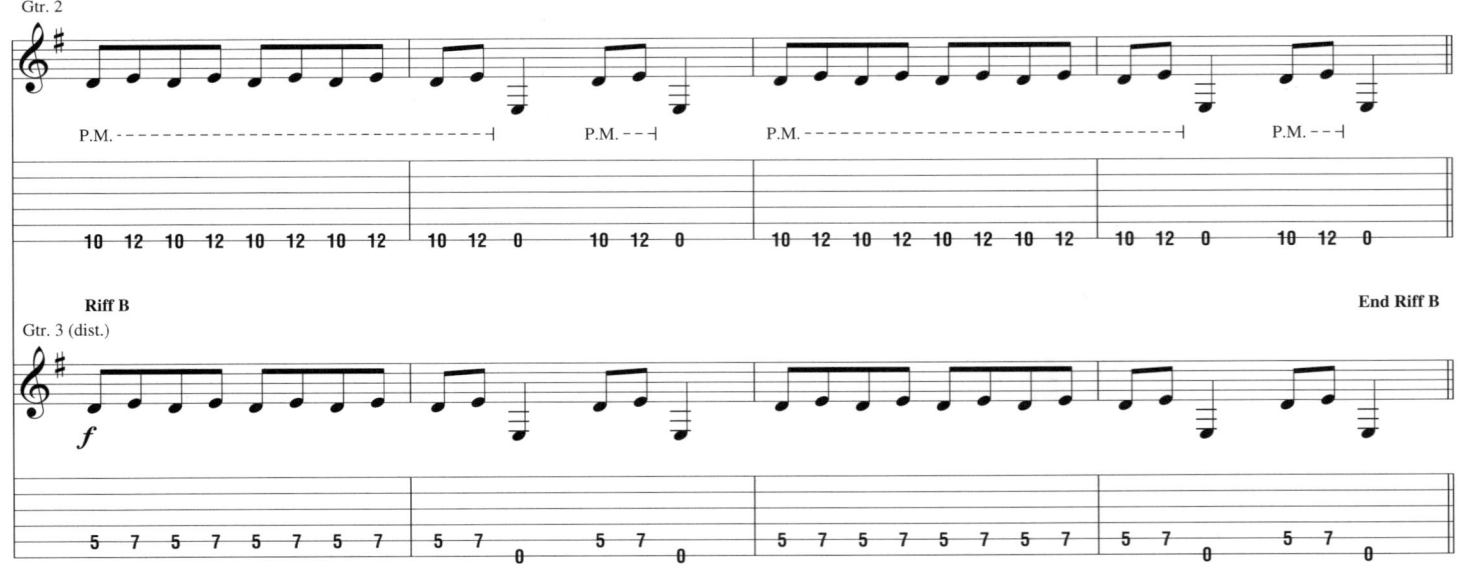

Copyright © 2011 SONGS OF UNIVERSAL, INC., MJ TWELVE MUSIC, LIVING UNDER A ROCK MUSIC,
I LOVE THE PUNK ROCK MUSIC, FLYING EARFORM MUSIC and RUTHENSMEAR MUSIC
All Rights for MJ TWELVE MUSIC and I LOVE THE PUNK ROCK MUSIC Controlled and Administered by SONGS OF UNIVERSAL, INC.
All Rights for LIVING UNDER A ROCK MUSIC Controlled and Administered by UNIVERSAL MUSIC CORP.
All Rights for FLYING EARFORM MUSIC and RUTHENSMEAR MUSIC Administered by BUG MUSIC
All Rights Reserved   Used by Permission

Gtr. 3: w/ Riff B (2 times)
*Gtrs. 2 & 4
Riff C
End Riff C
P.M.
*Gtr. 4 (dist.), played f.
Verse
E5 E♭5 D5 D♭5 C5 G A D5
1. These are my fa - mous last words!
Gtr. 4
Rhy. Fig. 1
**Gtrs. 2 & 3
End Rhy. Fig. 1
**Composite arrangement
Gtrs. 2 & 3: w/ Rhy. Fig. 1
E5 E♭5 D5 D♭5 C5 G A D5
My num-ber's up, bridg - es well burned!
Gtr. 4

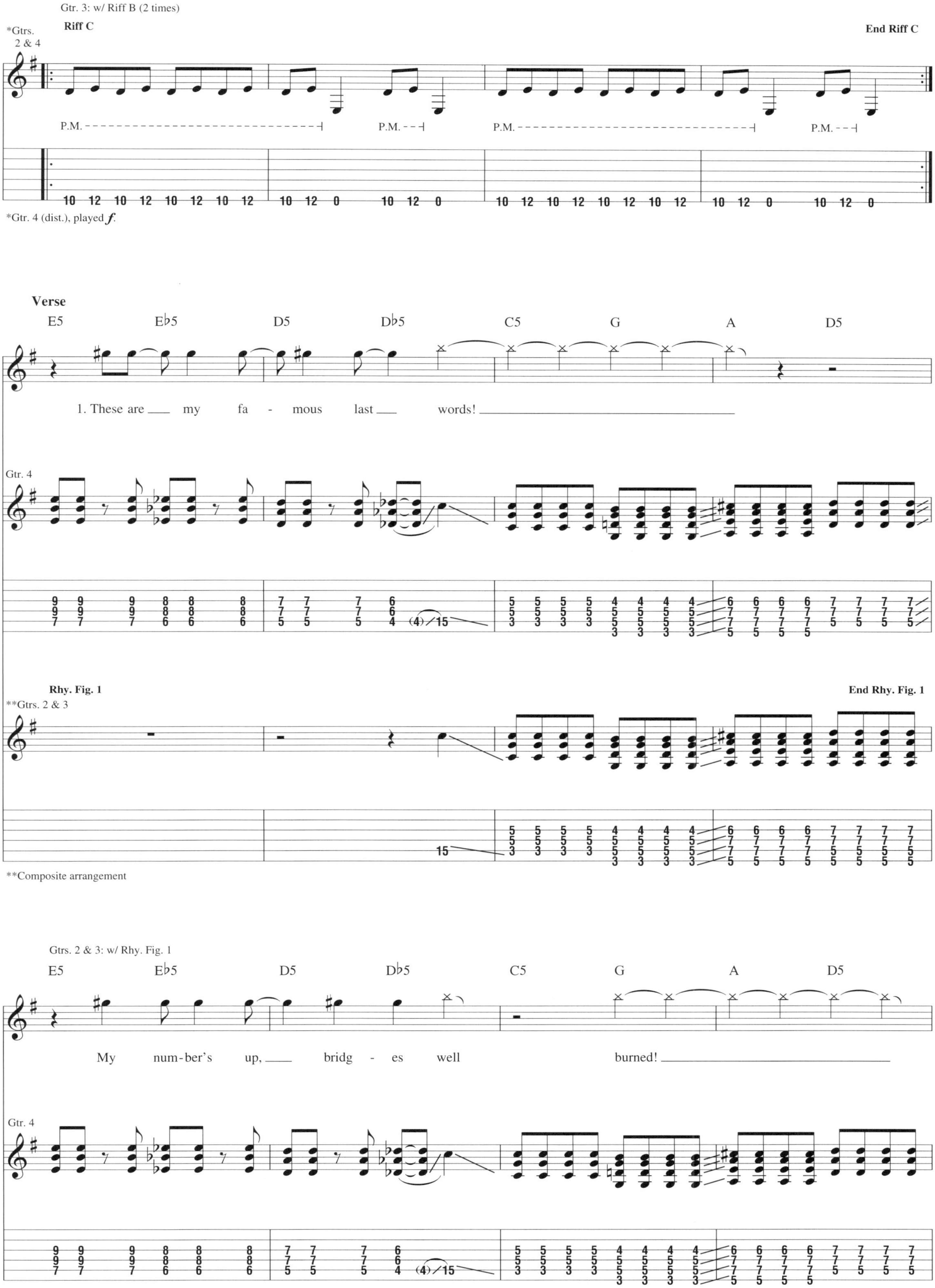

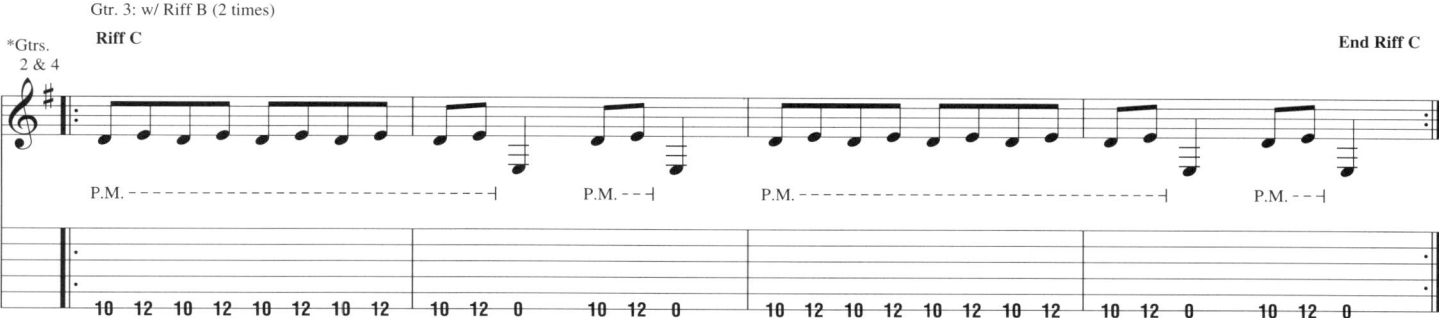

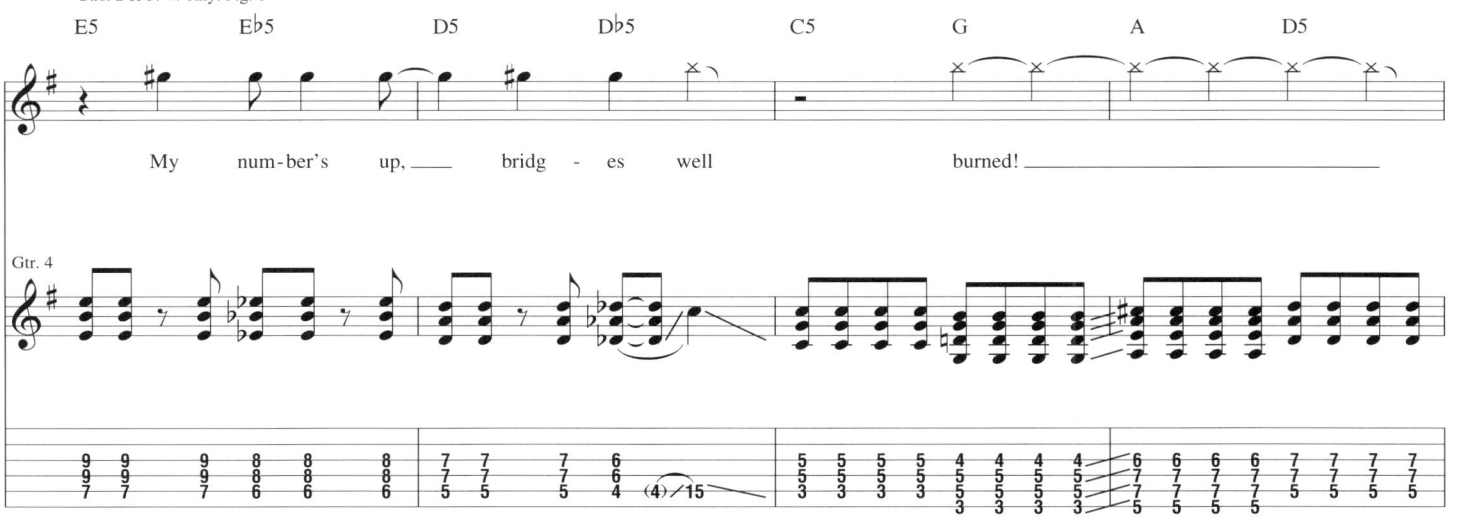

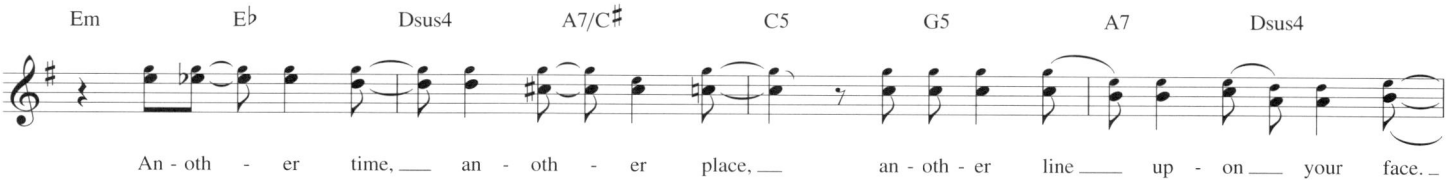

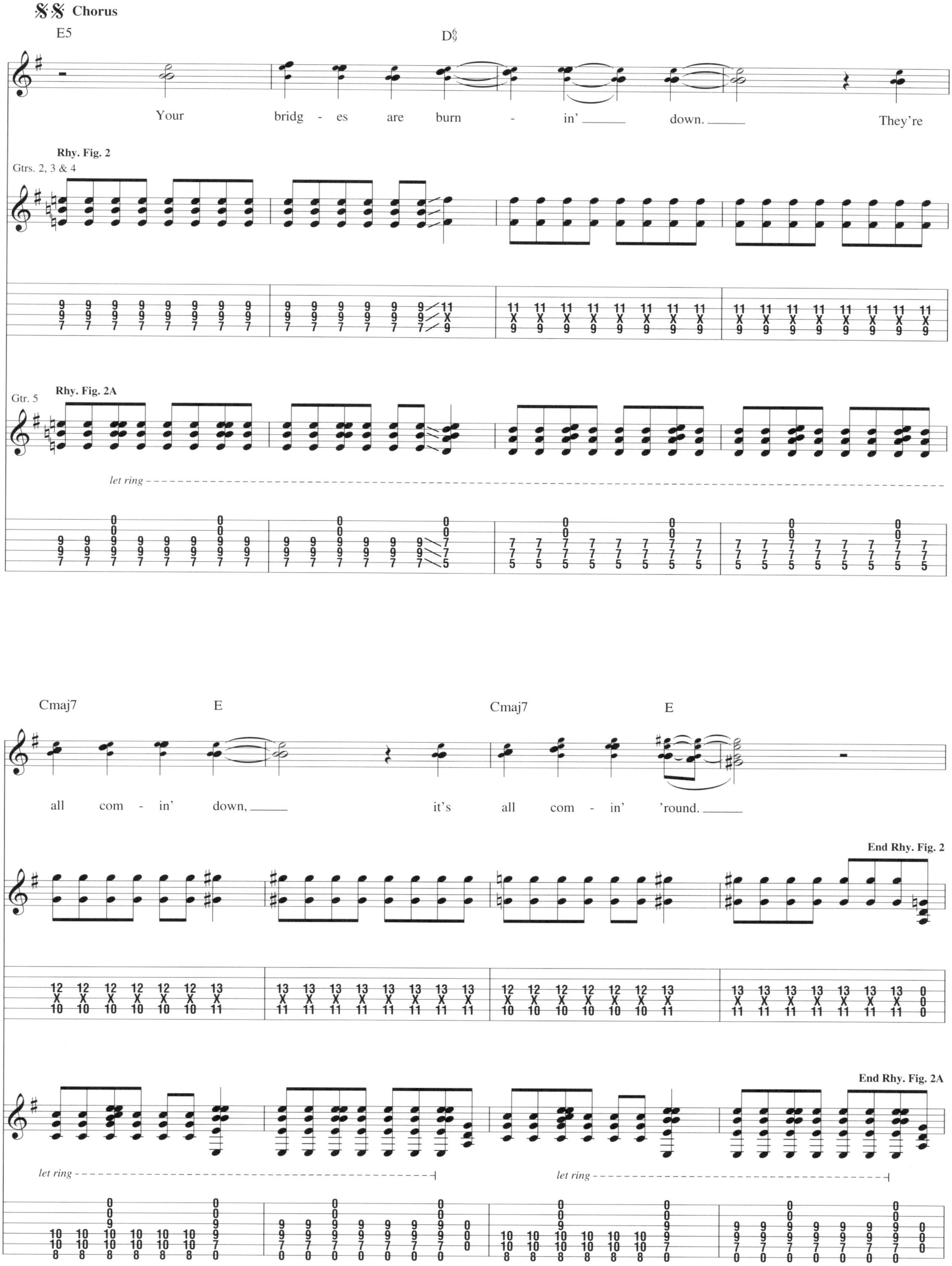
Chorus
E5
D6/9
Your bridg - es are burn - in' down. They're
Rhy. Fig. 2
Gtrs. 2, 3 & 4
Gtr. 5
Rhy. Fig. 2A
let ring
Cmaj7
E
Cmaj7
E
all com - in' down, it's all com - in' 'round.
End Rhy. Fig. 2
End Rhy. Fig. 2A
let ring
let ring

Gtrs. 2, 3 & 4: w/ Rhy. Fig. 2 (1st 4 meas.)
Gtr. 5: w/ Rhy. Fig. 2A
E5
D6/9
You're burn - in' them down. It's
To Coda 2
To Coda 1
Cmaj7
E
all com - in' 'round, they're all com - in' down. You're
Riff E
End Riff E
Gtrs. 2, 3 & 4
Cmaj7
E
D5
E♭5
bridg - es are burn - in' down.
Rhy. Fig. 3
End Rhy. Fig. 3
Gtrs. 2, 3 & 4
Gtr. 5
Rhy. Fig. 3A
End Rhy. Fig. 3A
let ring

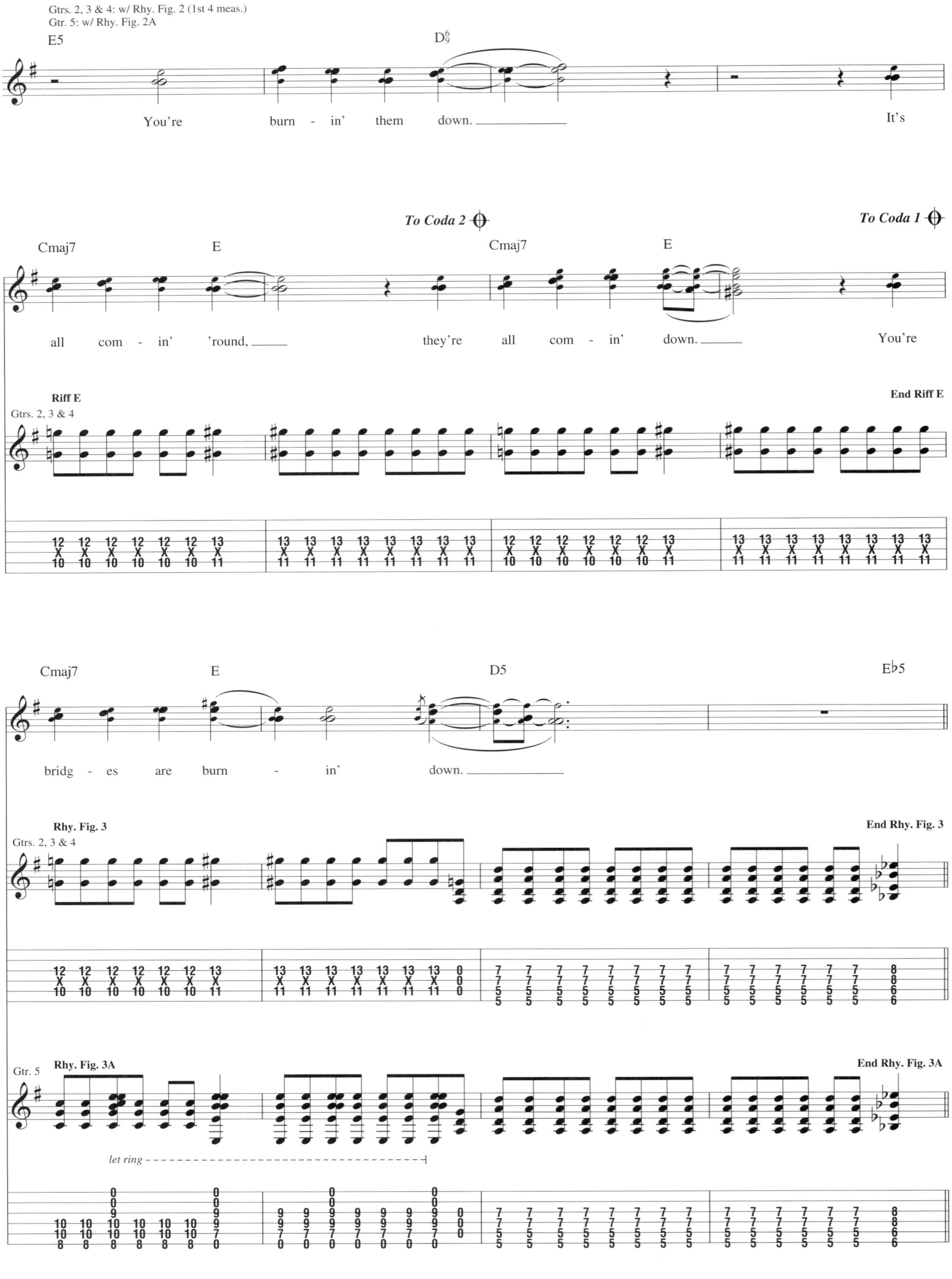

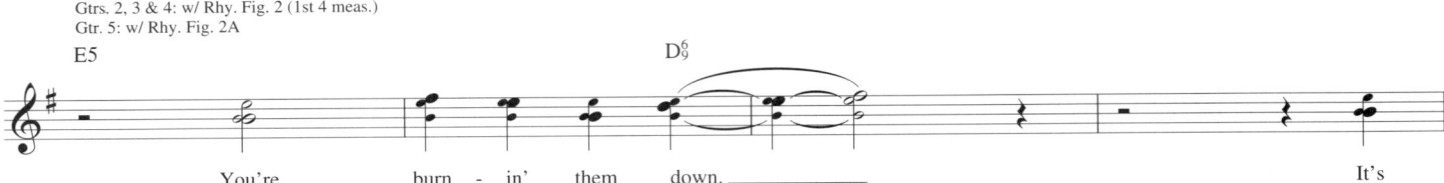

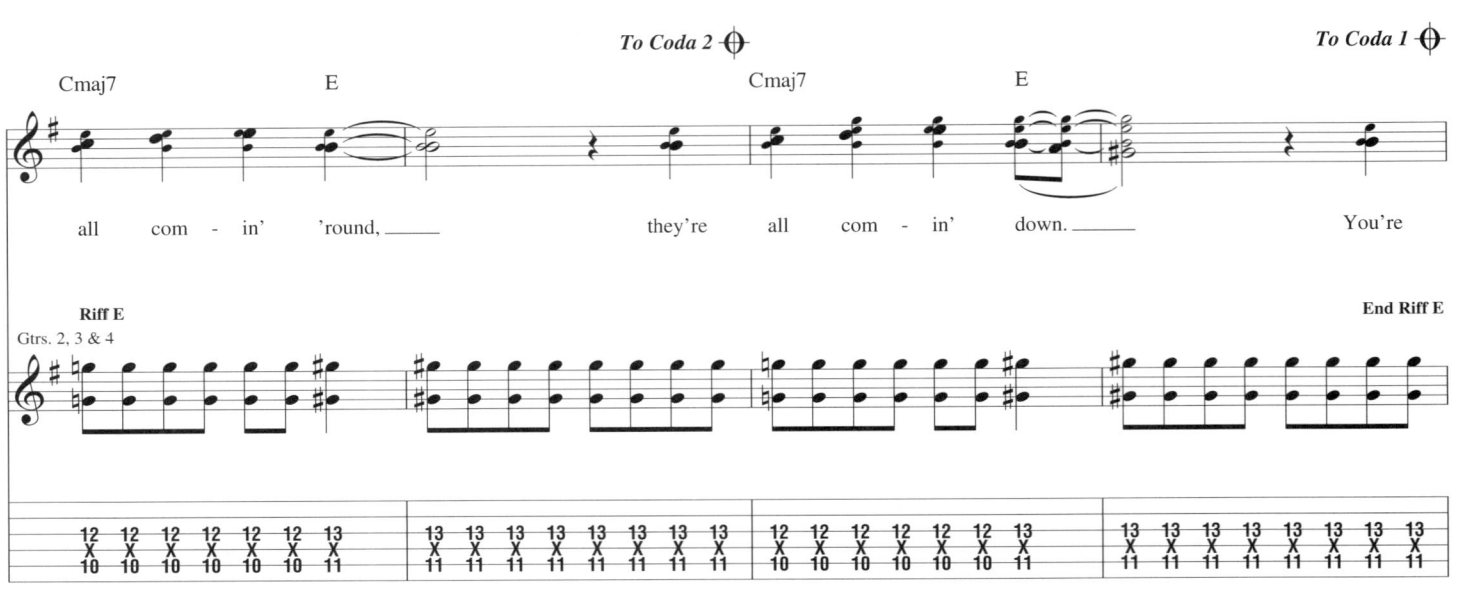

Rope

Words and Music by David Grohl, Taylor Hawkins, Christopher Shiflett, Nate Mendel and Pat Smear

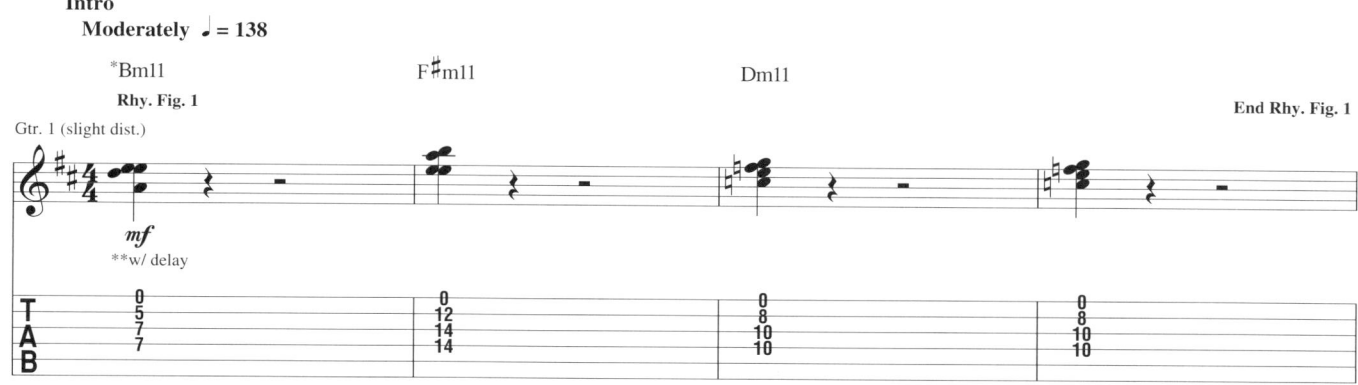

*Chord symbols reflect implied harmony.
**Delay set for quarter-note triplet regeneration w/ 5 repeats.

Copyright © 2011 SONGS OF UNIVERSAL, INC., MJ TWELVE MUSIC, LIVING UNDER A ROCK MUSIC,
I LOVE THE PUNK ROCK MUSIC, FLYING EARFORM MUSIC and RUTHENSMEAR MUSIC
All Rights for MJ TWELVE MUSIC and I LOVE THE PUNK ROCK MUSIC Controlled and Administered by SONGS OF UNIVERSAL, INC.
All Rights for LIVING UNDER A ROCK MUSIC Controlled and Administered by UNIVERSAL MUSIC CORP.
All Rights for FLYING EARFORM MUSIC and RUTHENSMEAR MUSIC Administered by BUG MUSIC
All Rights Reserved   Used by Permission

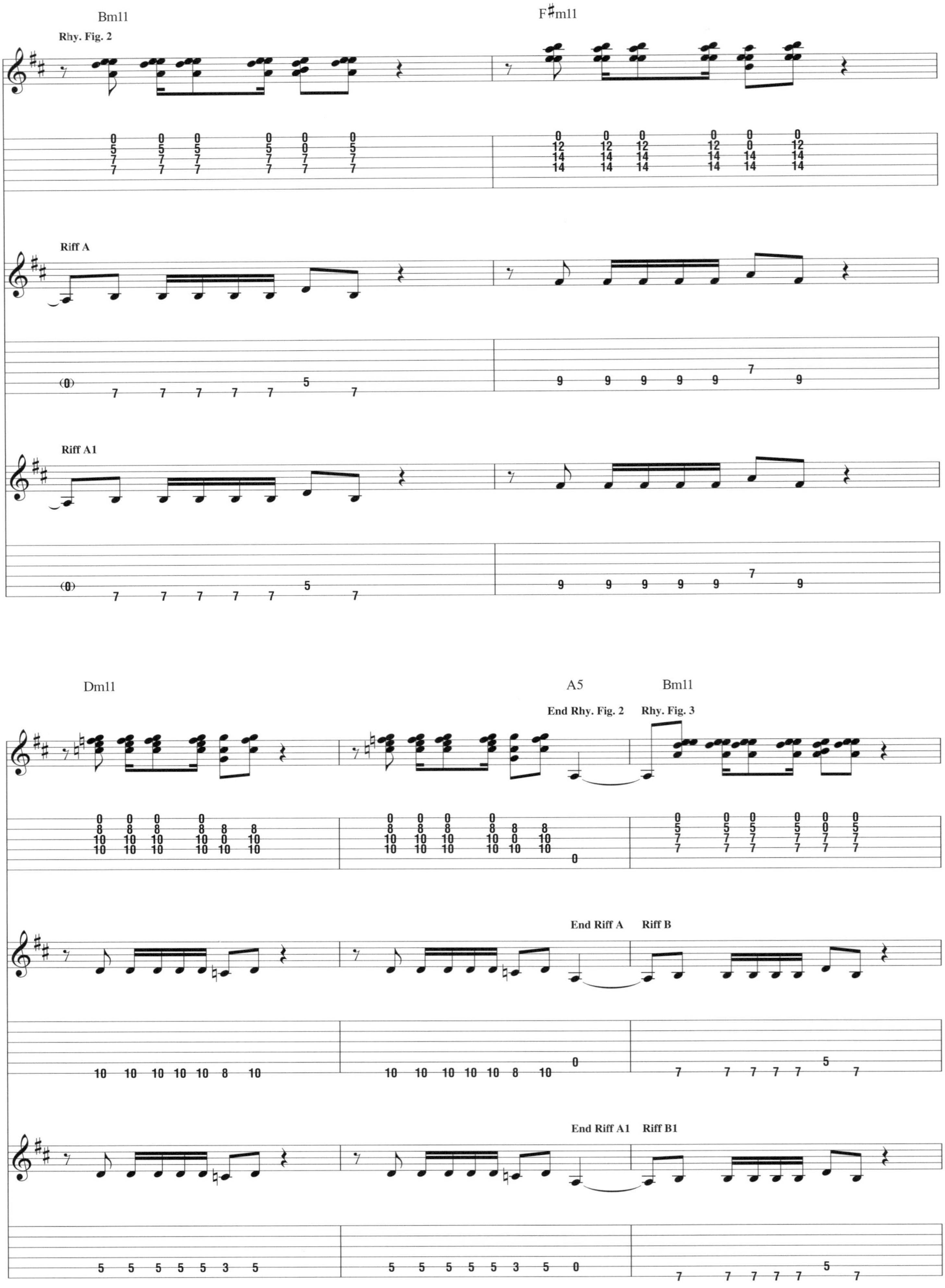
Bm11
F♯m11
Rhy. Fig. 2
Riff A
Riff A1
Dm11
A5
Bm11
End Rhy. Fig. 2
Rhy. Fig. 3
End Riff A
Riff B
End Riff A1
Riff B1

F#m11
*Dm11
A5
End Rhy. Fig. 3
End Riff B
End Riff B1
*Bass plays F.
Verse
Bm11
F#m11
Dm11
A5
1. This in - de - ci - sion got me climb - in' up a wall.
**Gtr. 2
Rhy. Fig. 4
End Rhy. Fig. 4
**Doubled throughout
Riff C
Gtrs. 1 & 3

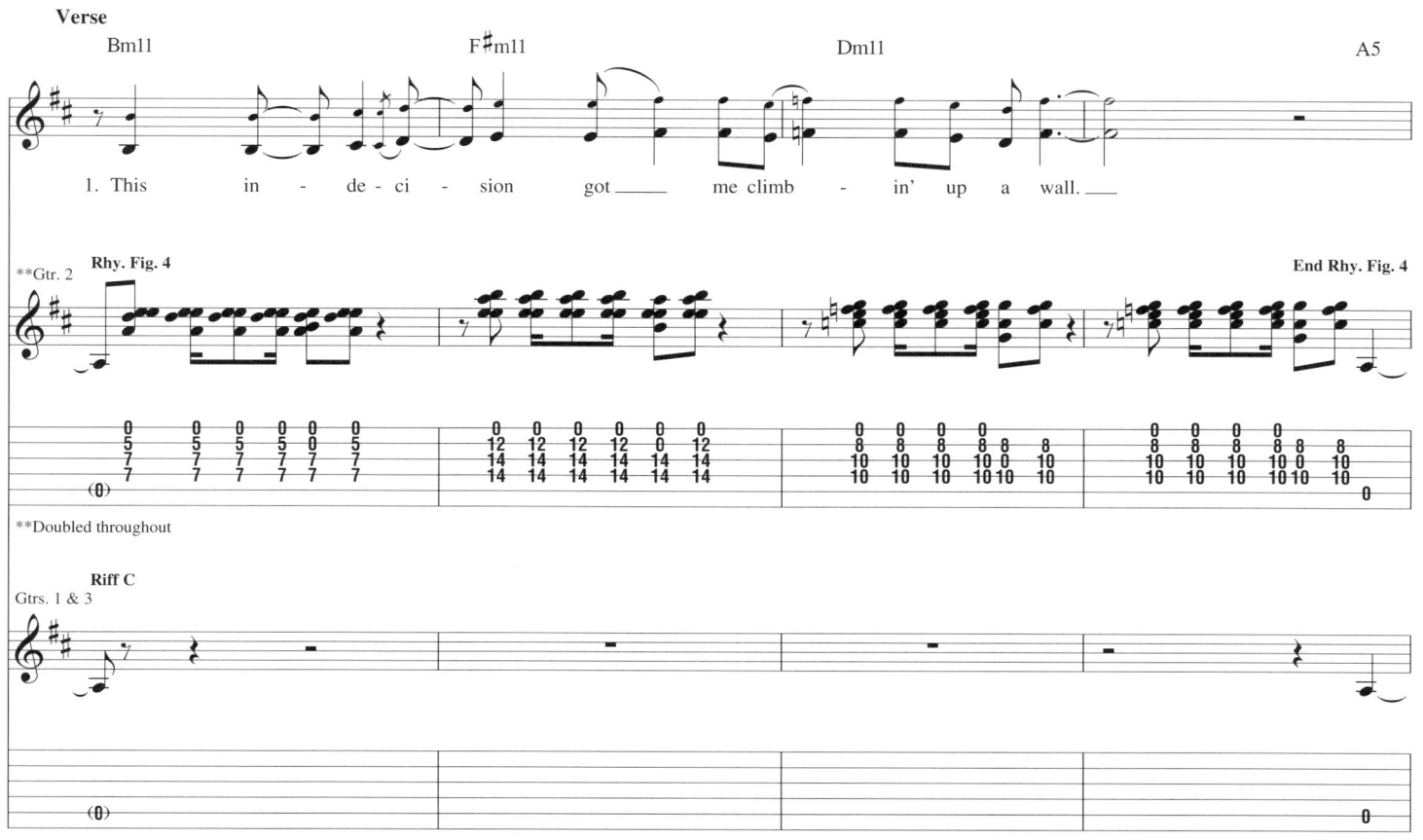

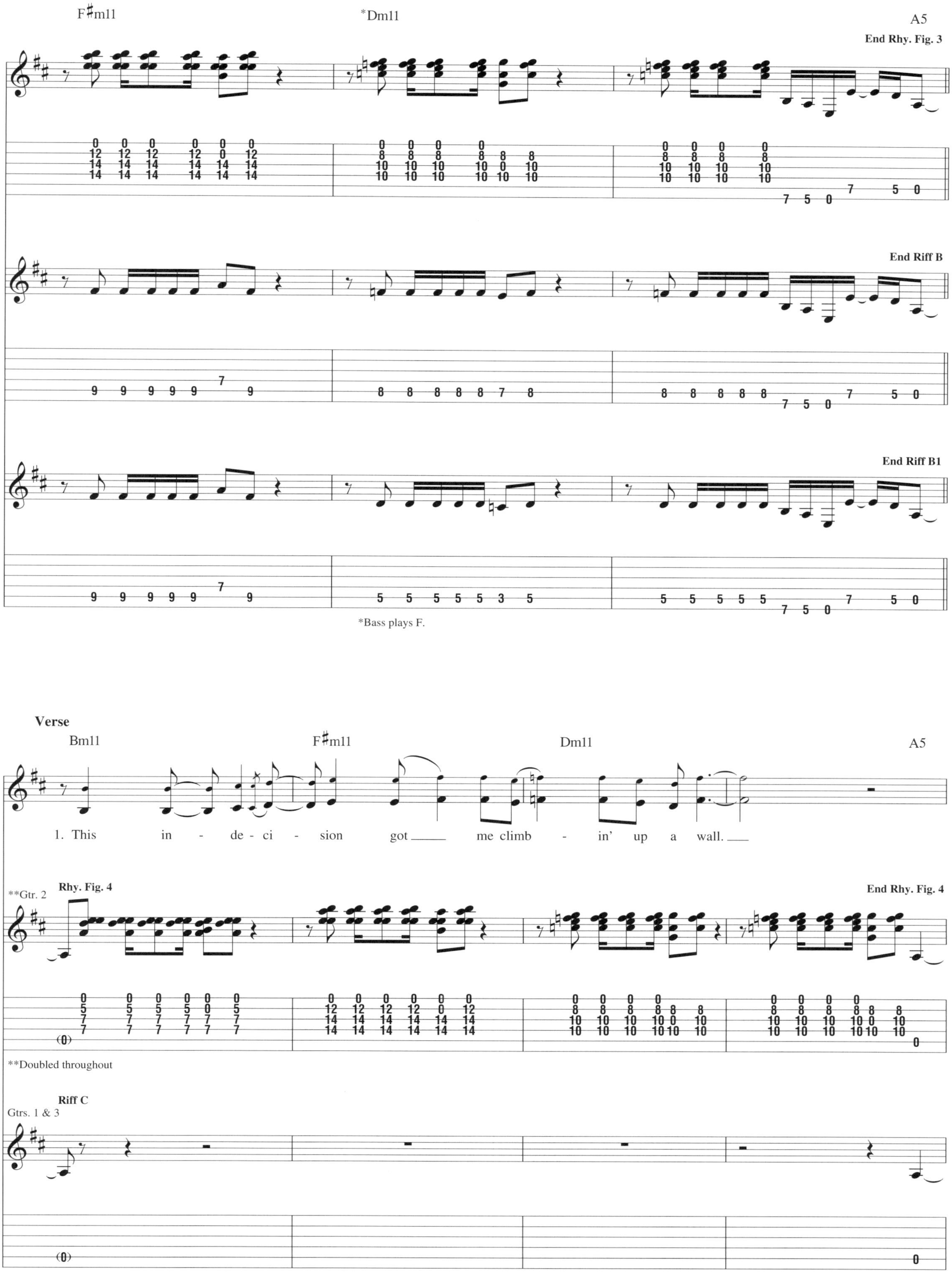

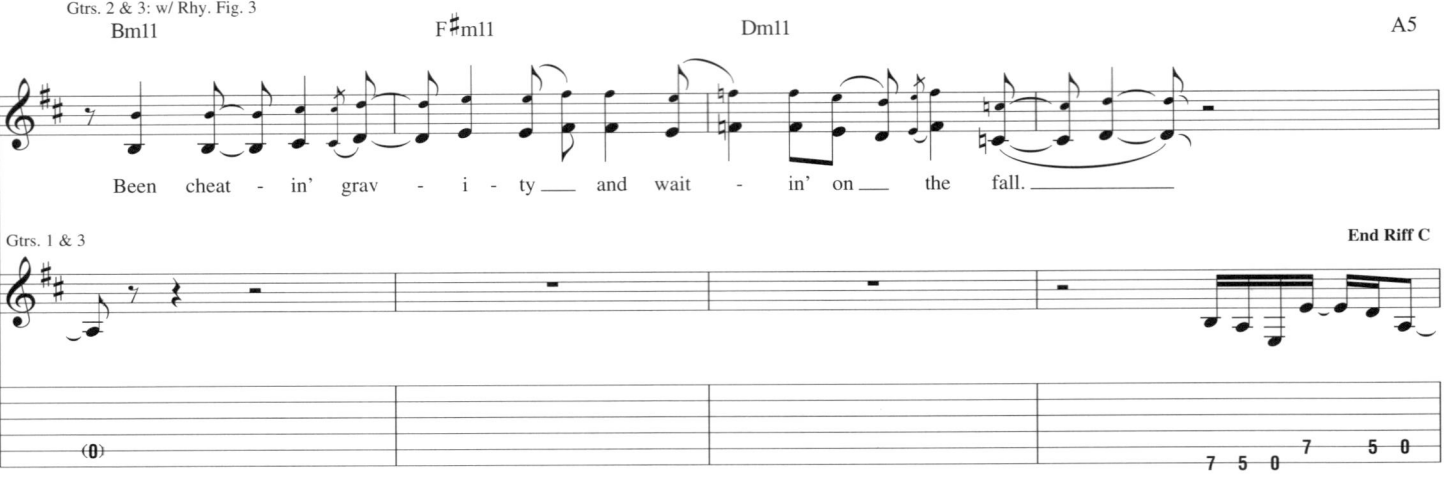

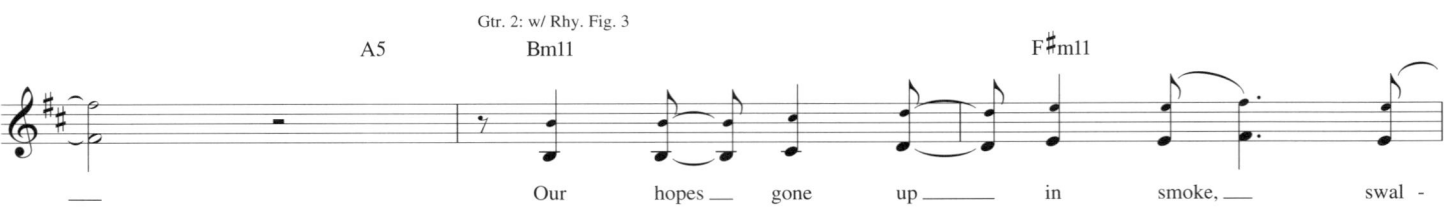

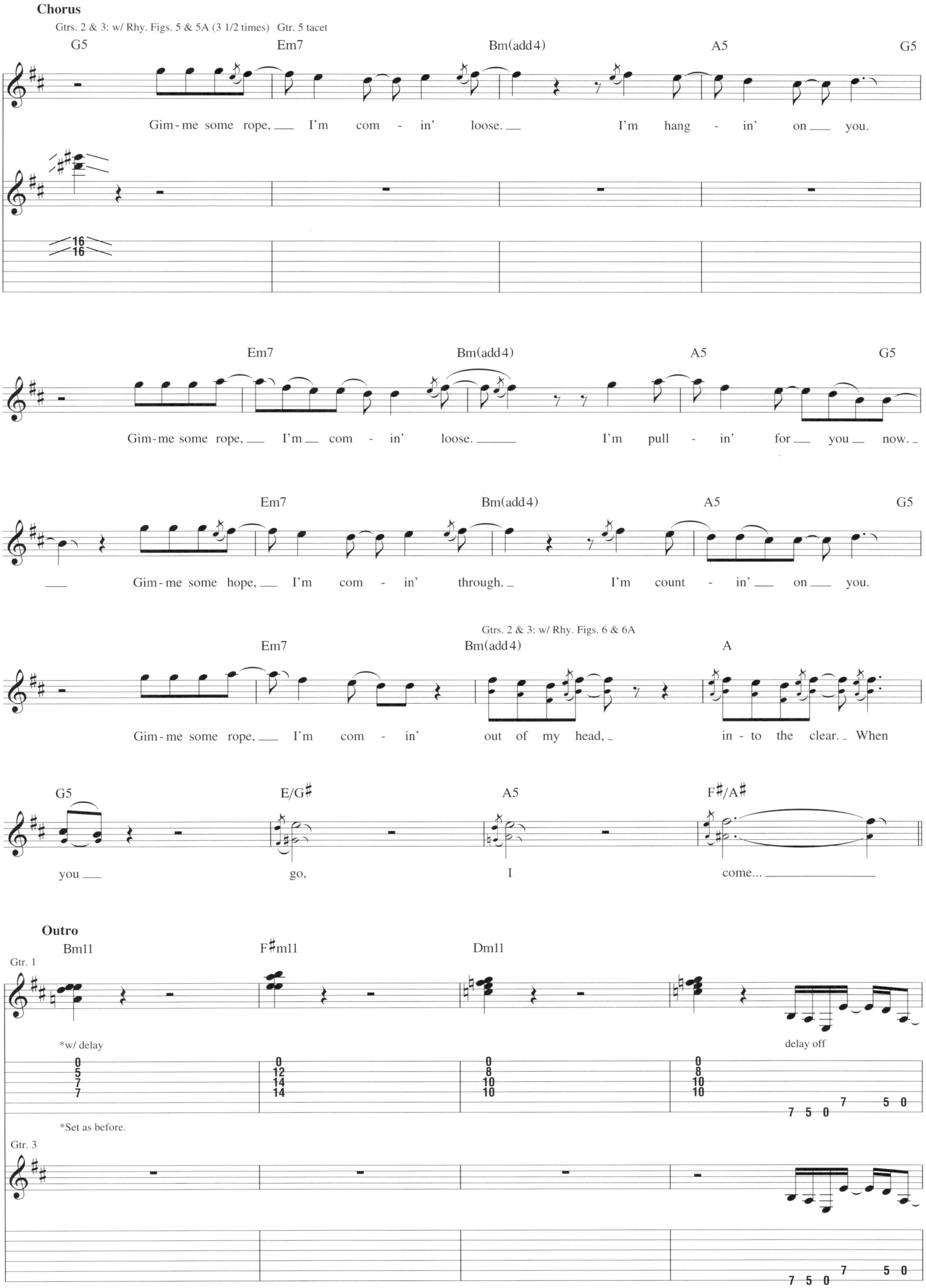
Chorus
Gtrs. 2 & 3: w/ Rhy. Figs. 5 & 5A (3 1/2 times) Gtr. 5 tacet
G5 Em7 Bm(add4) A5 G5
Gim-me some rope, I'm com - in' loose. I'm hang - in' on you.
Em7 Bm(add4) A5 G5
Gim-me some rope, I'm com - in' loose. I'm pull - in' for you now.
Em7 Bm(add4) A5 G5
Gim-me some hope, I'm com - in' through. I'm count - in' on you.
Gtrs. 2 & 3: w/ Rhy. Figs. 6 & 6A
Em7 Bm(add4) A
Gim-me some rope, I'm com - in' out of my head, in - to the clear. When
G5 E/G# A5 F#/A#
you go, I come...
Outro
Bm11 F#m11 Dm11
Gtr. 1
*w/ delay
delay off
*Set as before.
Gtr. 3

Bm7add4
F♯m7add4
loose.
Gtr. 2
Gtr. 1
Gtr. 3
Dm11

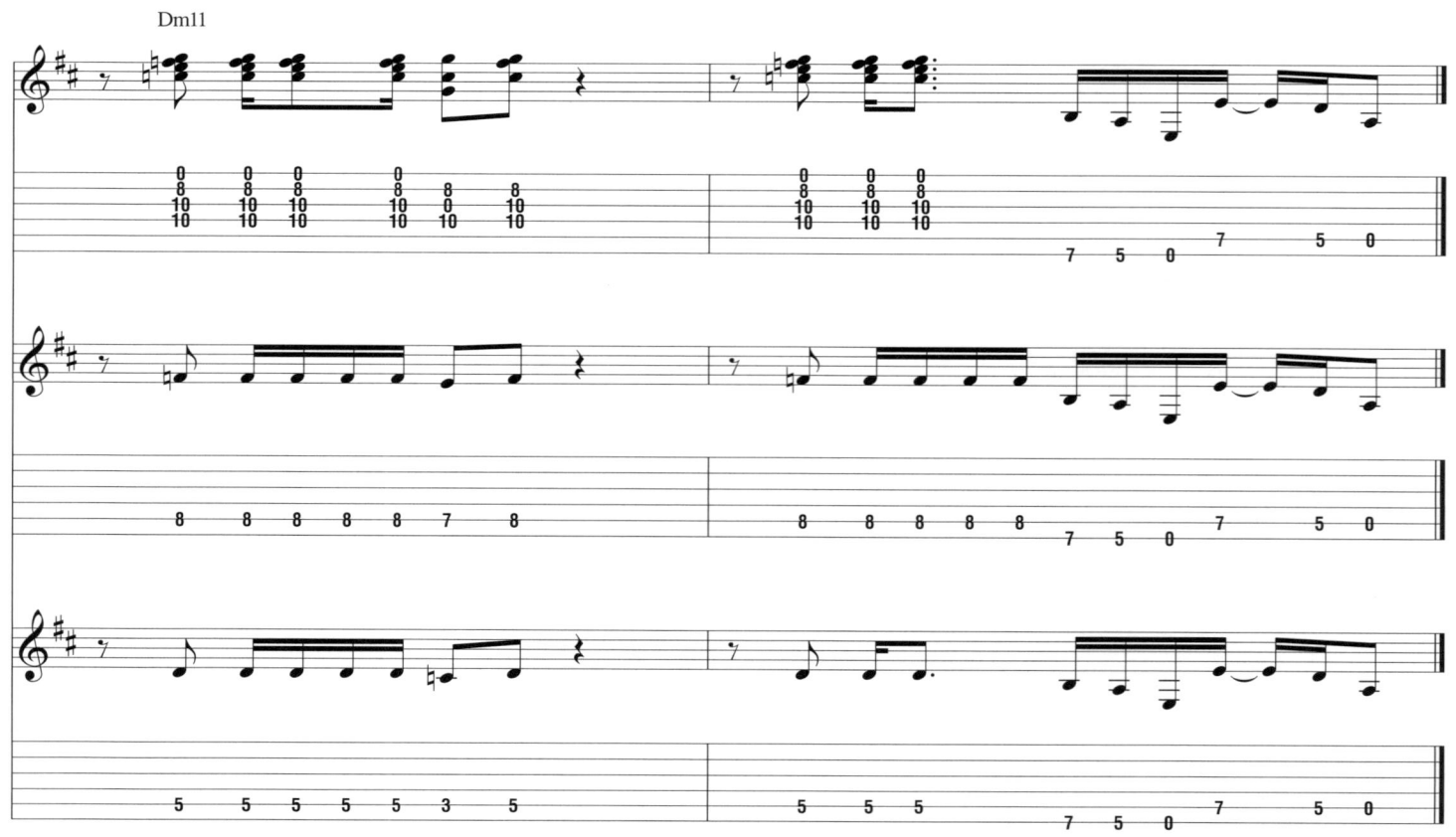

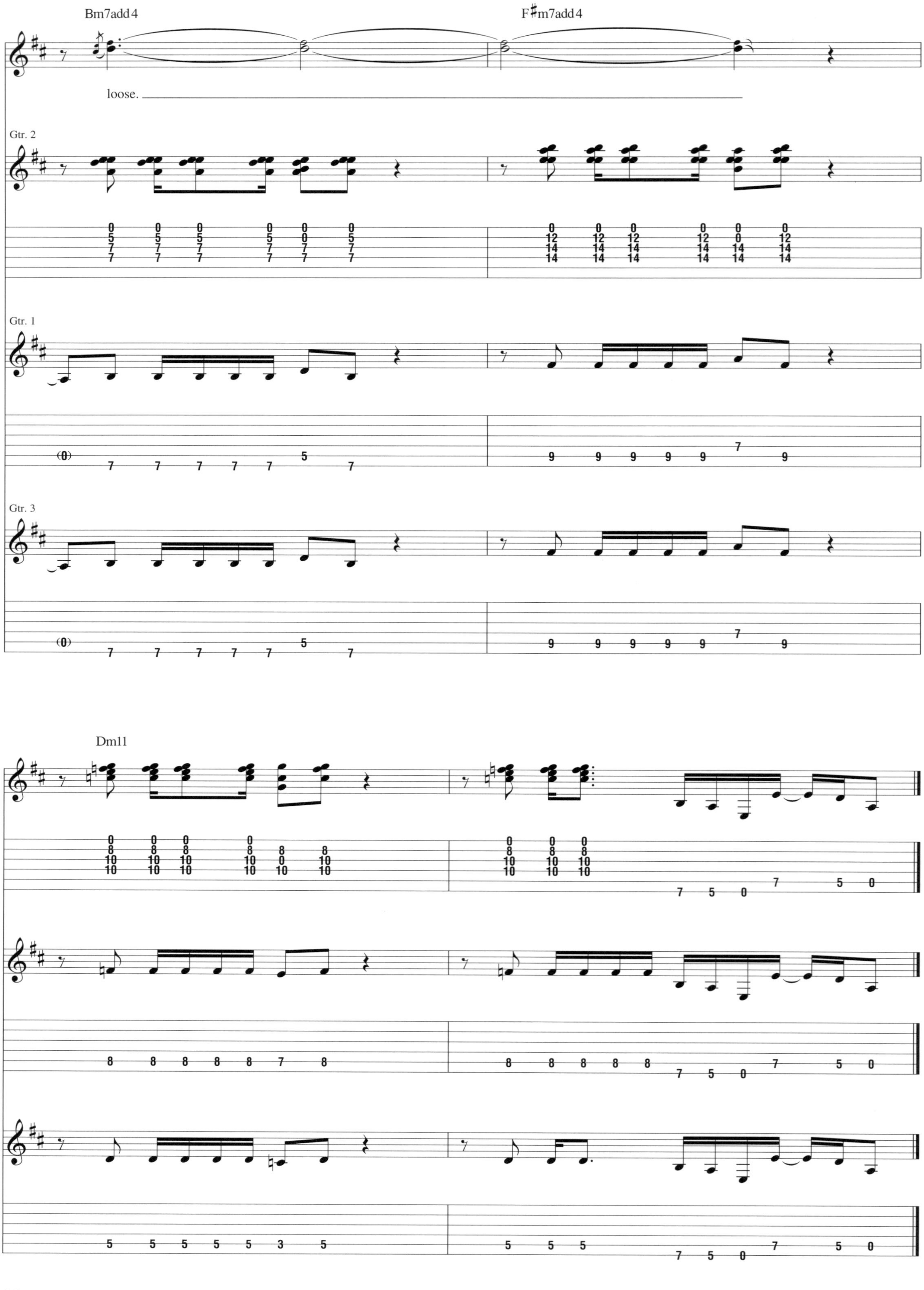

Dear Rosemary

Words and Music by David Grohl, Taylor Hawkins, Christopher Shiflett, Nate Mendel and Pat Smear

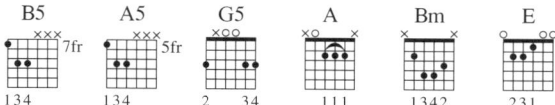

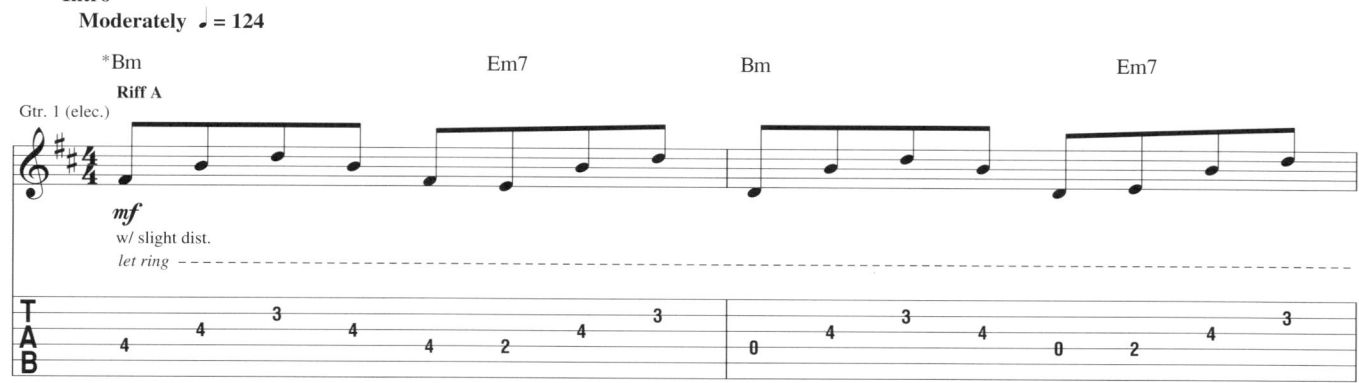

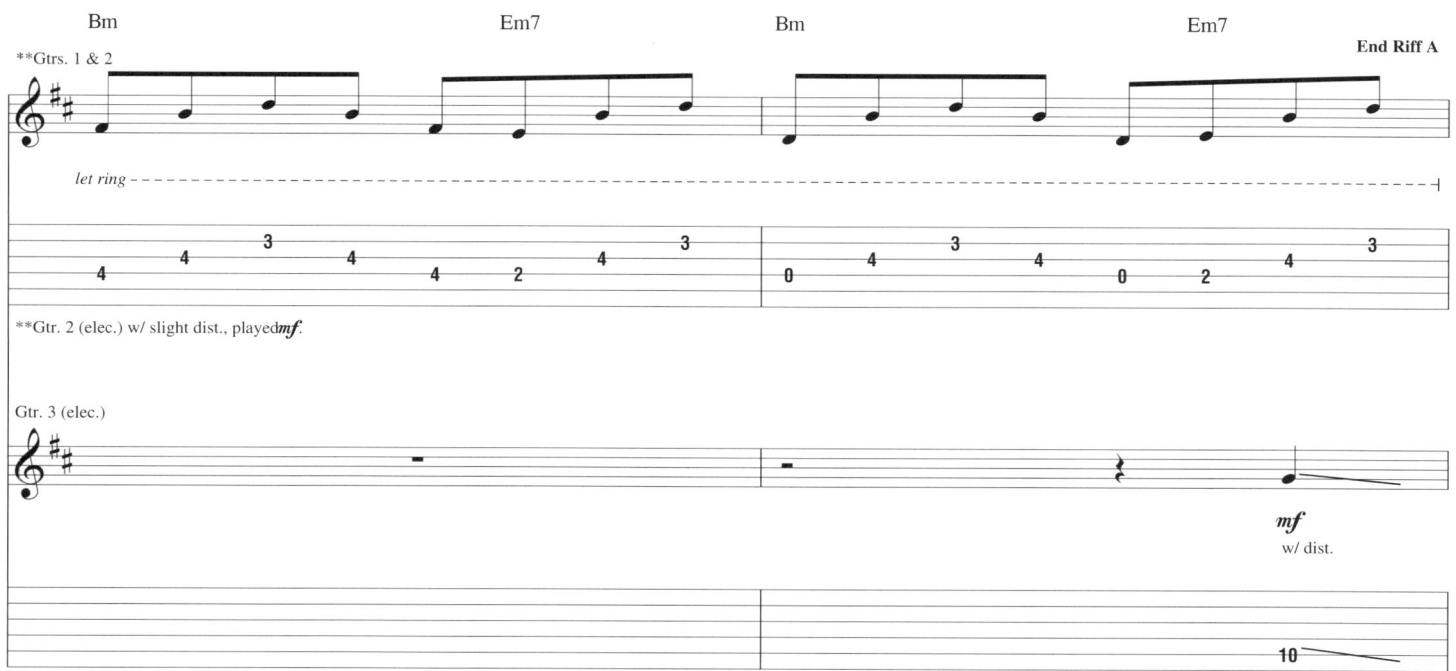

*Chord symbols reflect implied harmony.

**Gtr. 2 (elec.) w/ slight dist., played mf.

Copyright © 2011 SONGS OF UNIVERSAL, INC., MJ TWELVE MUSIC, LIVING UNDER A ROCK MUSIC,
I LOVE THE PUNK ROCK MUSIC, FLYING EARFORM MUSIC and RUTHENSMEAR MUSIC
All Rights for MJ TWELVE MUSIC and I LOVE THE PUNK ROCK MUSIC Controlled and Administered by SONGS OF UNIVERSAL, INC.
All Rights for LIVING UNDER A ROCK MUSIC Controlled and Administered by UNIVERSAL MUSIC CORP.
All Rights for FLYING EARFORM MUSIC and RUTHENSMEAR MUSIC Administered by BUG MUSIC
All Rights Reserved   Used by Permission

*See top of first page of song for chord diagrams pertaining to rhythm slashes.

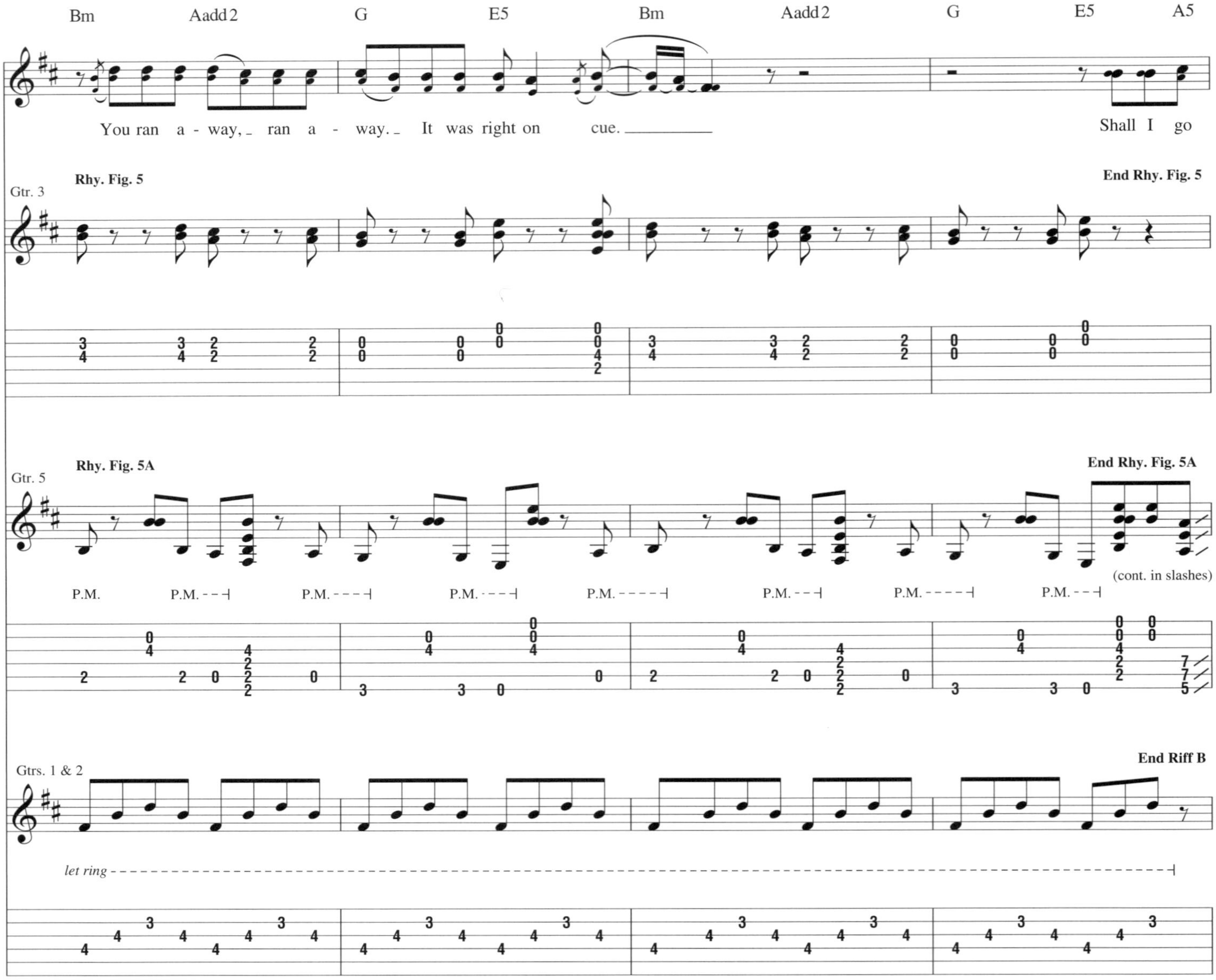

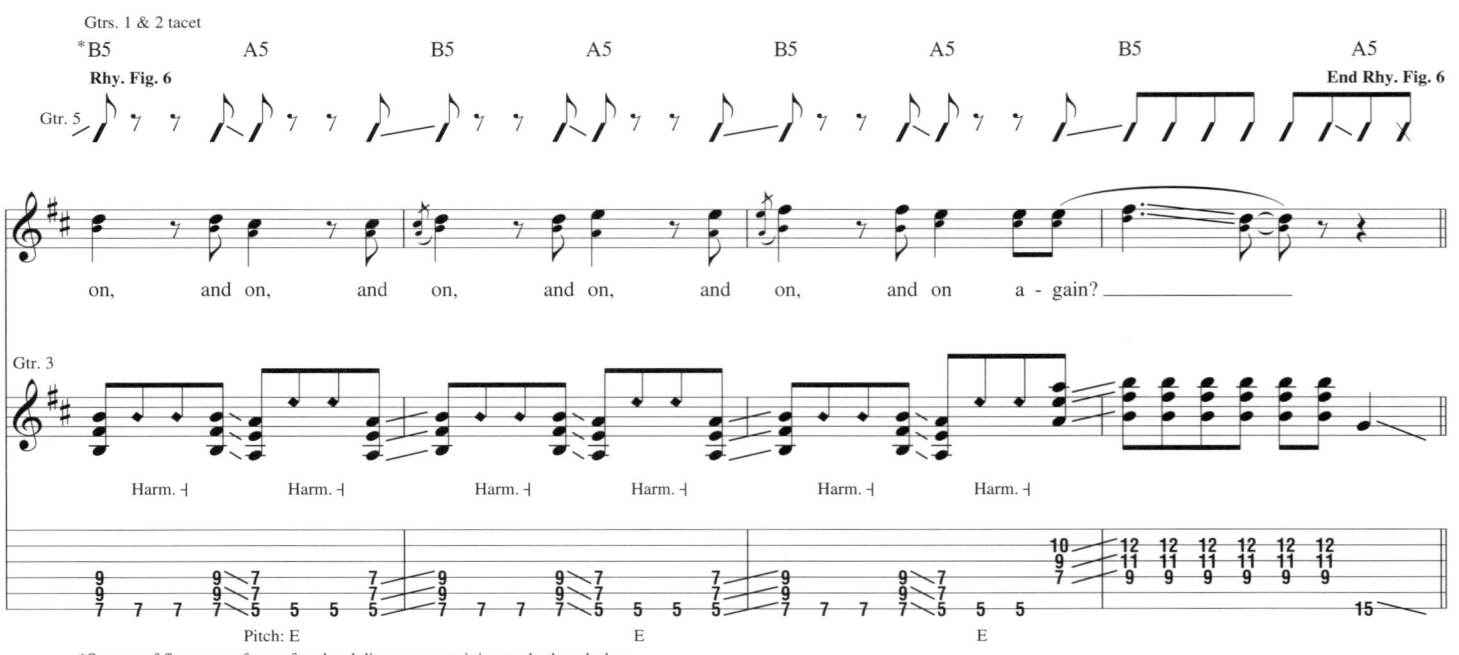

Gtrs. 3 & 5: w/ Rhy. Fig. 1 (4 times)

| Bm | Aadd$\frac{2}{4}$ | G | Em7 | Bm | Aadd$\frac{2}{4}$ | G | Em7 |

-mar - y, _____ you're part of me. _____ Dear Rose-
(Dear Rose - mar - y, _____ you're part of me. _____

| Bm | Aadd$\frac{2}{4}$ | G | Em7 | Bm | Aadd$\frac{2}{4}$ | G | Em7 |

-mar - y, _____ please par - don me. _____
Dear Rose - mar - y, _____ please par - don me.) _____

White Limo

Words and Music by David Grohl, Taylor Hawkins, Christopher Shiflett, Nate Mendel and Pat Smear

*Chord symbols reflect implied harmony.

D Bb G B
Go! Go!
You said that I've been a - way so long.
You nev - er have been a - way so long.
Gtrs. 1 & 2
Rhy. Fig. 4
Gtr. 3
Rhy. Fig. 4A

To Coda
D A Em A5 B5 C5 B5 A5 C5
Go! Go! And the ride was shared. Go
End Rhy. Fig. 4
End Rhy. Fig. 4A

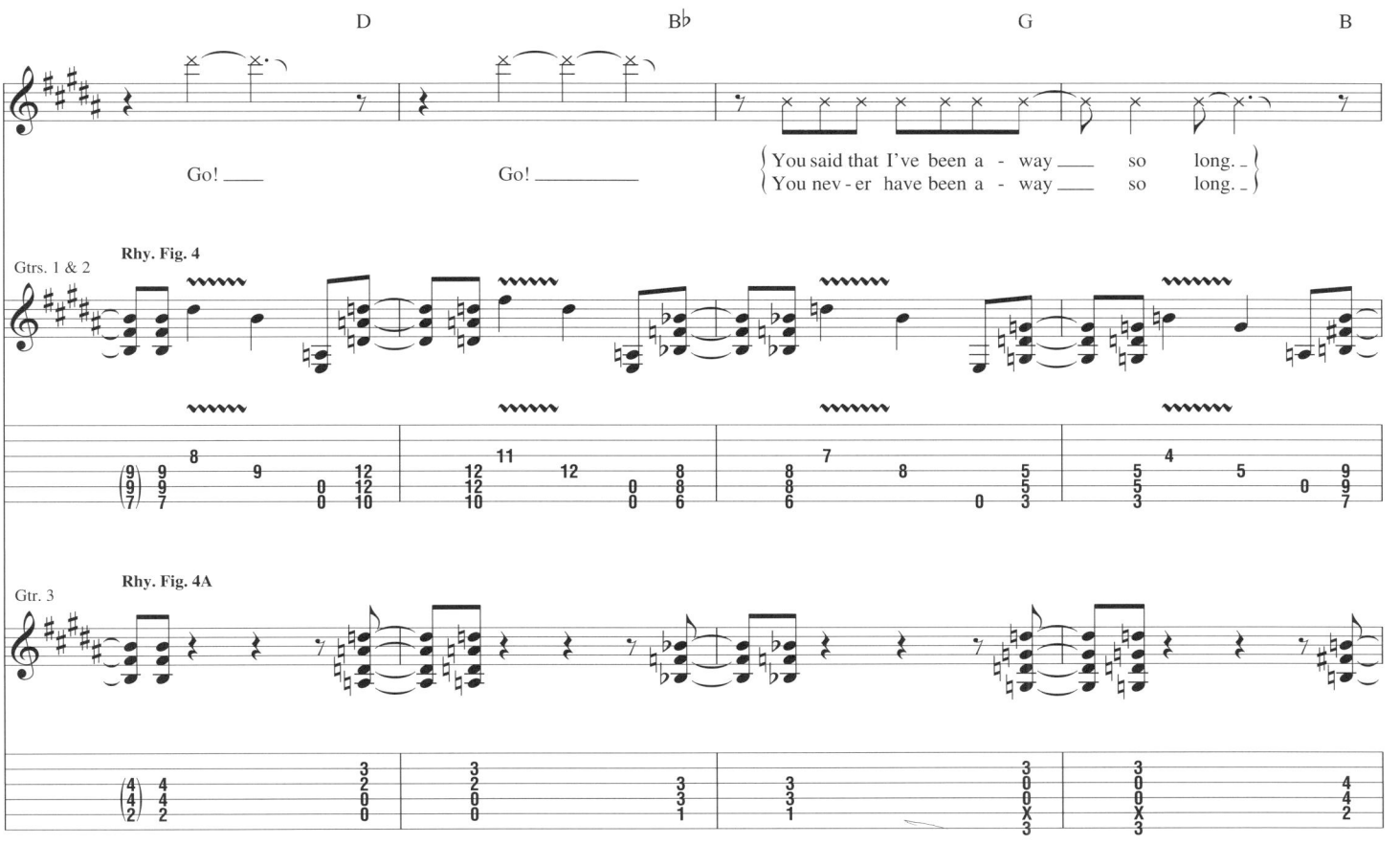

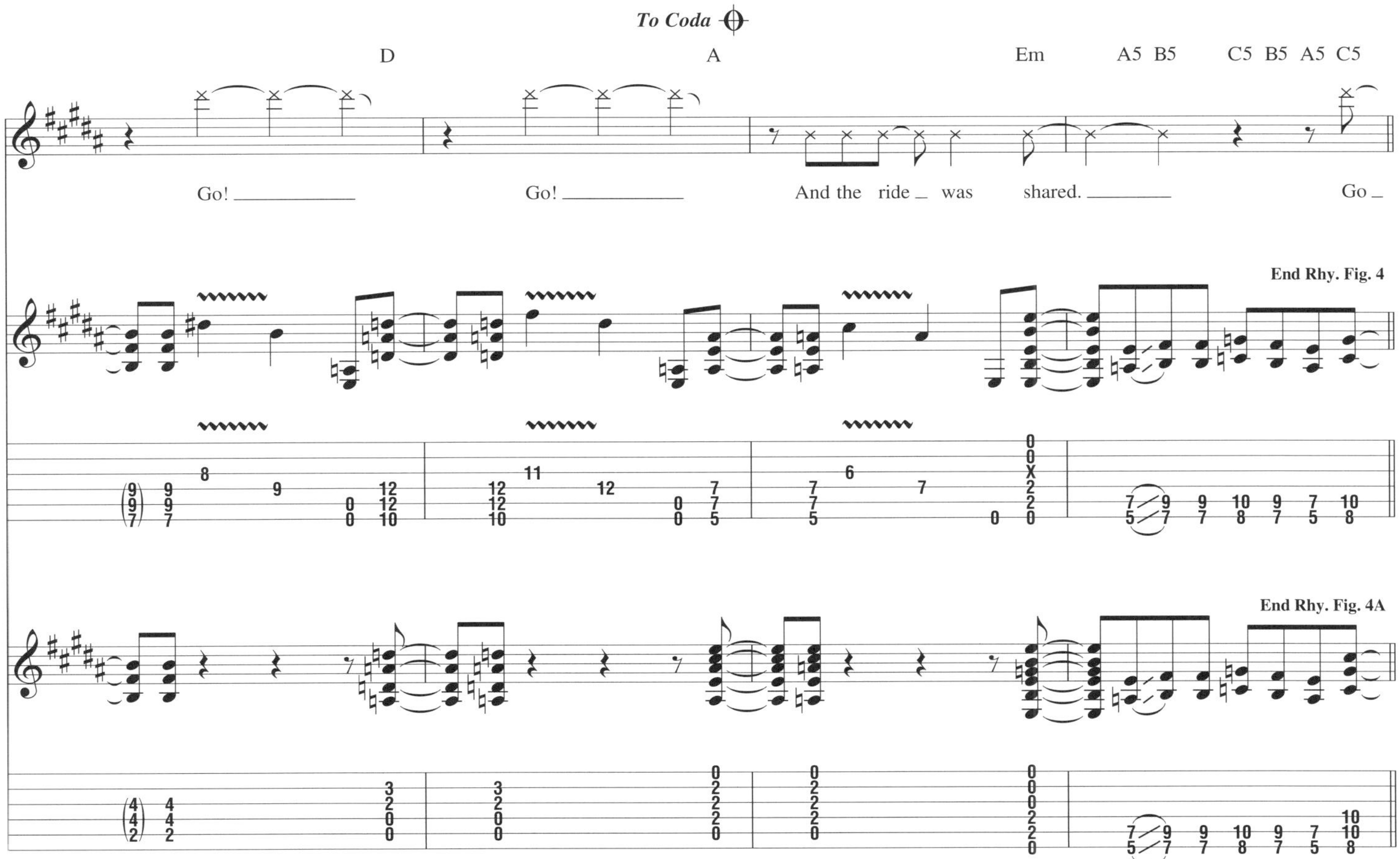

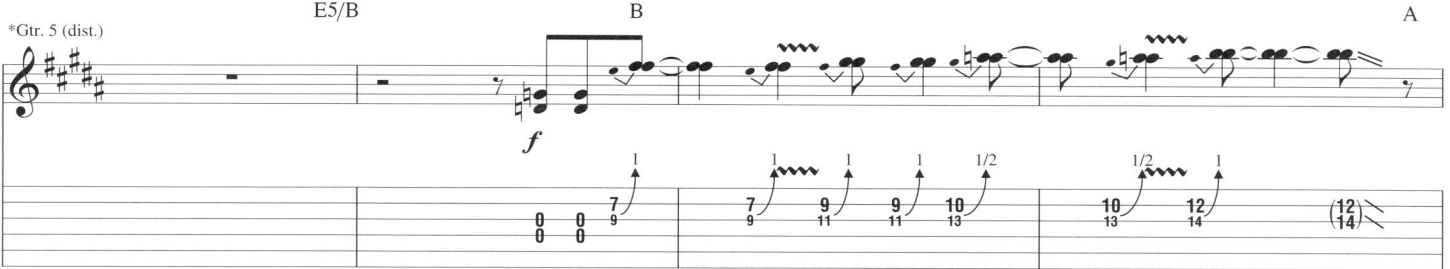
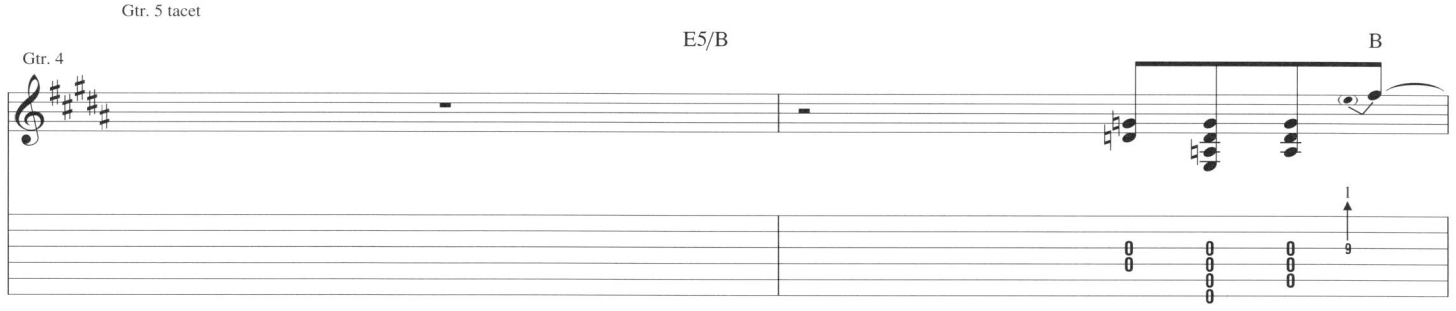
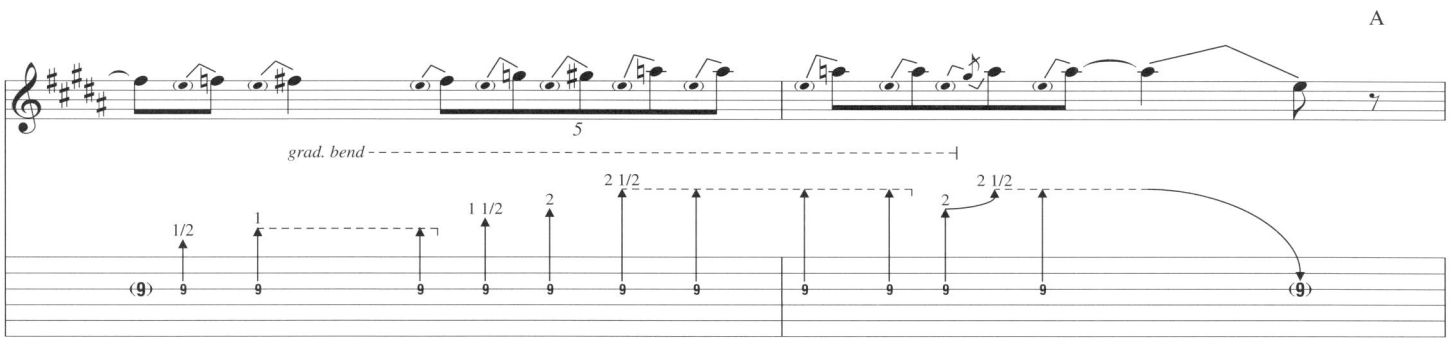
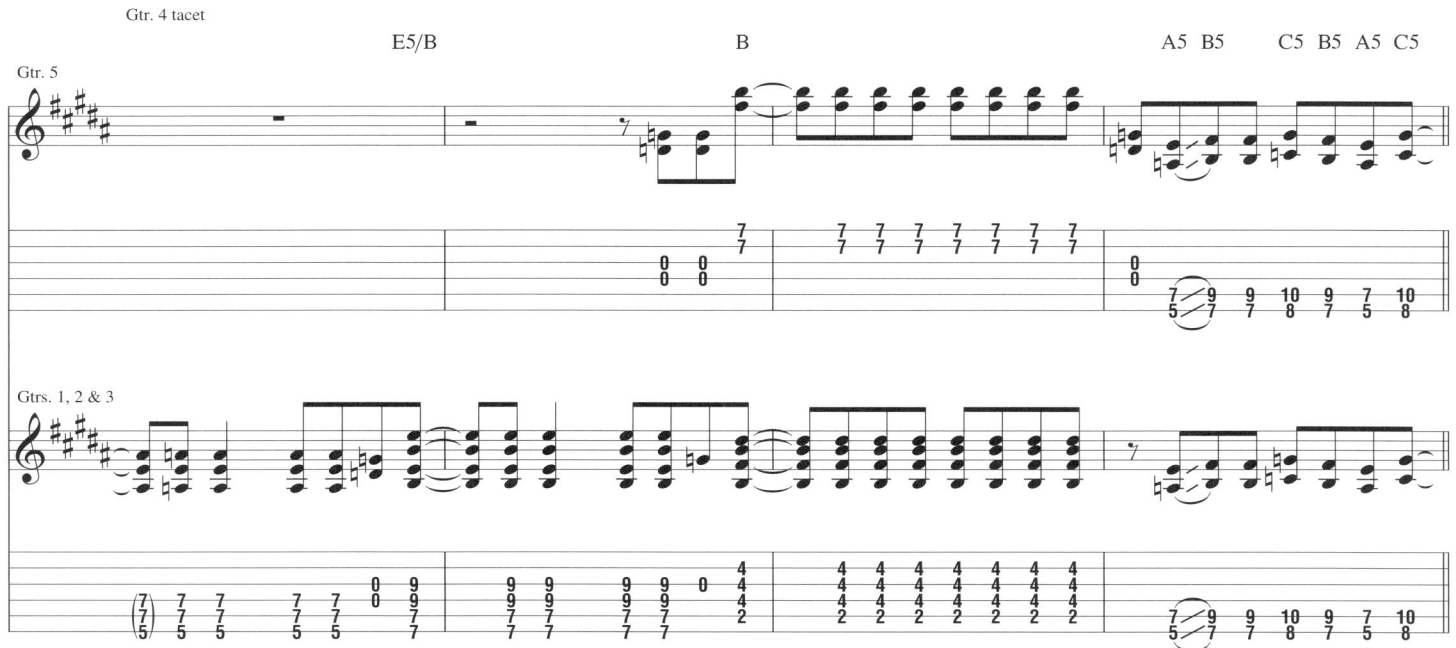

Interlude

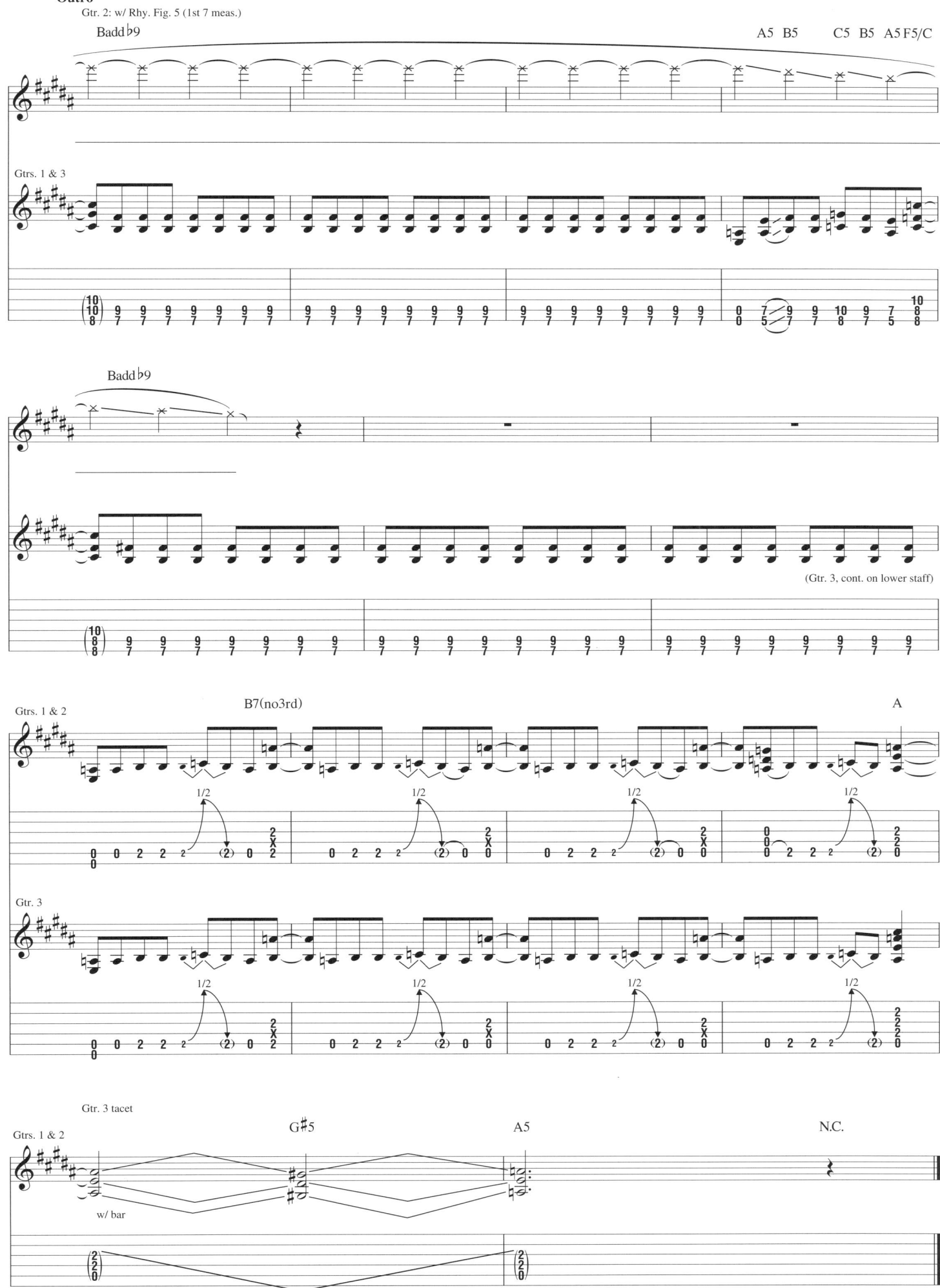

Arlandria

Words and Music by David Grohl, Taylor Hawkins, Christopher Shiflett, Nate Mendel and Pat Smear

*Doubled throughout
**Chord symbols reflect implied harmony.

C♯m7
Asus2
E5
F♯
Shame, shame, go a - way.
Come a - gain some oth - er day.
Gtr. 2
End Riff A
let ring
Gtr. 4
mf
Gtr. 1
*Gtr. 5 (dist.)
f
*Doubled throughout
Pre-Chorus
Gtrs. 1, 2 & 4 tacet
C♯5
A5
E5
B5
F♯5
You used to say I could-n't save you e-nough, so I've been sav - in' it up, I start-ed sav - in' it up.
Gtr. 5
Rhy. Fig. 3

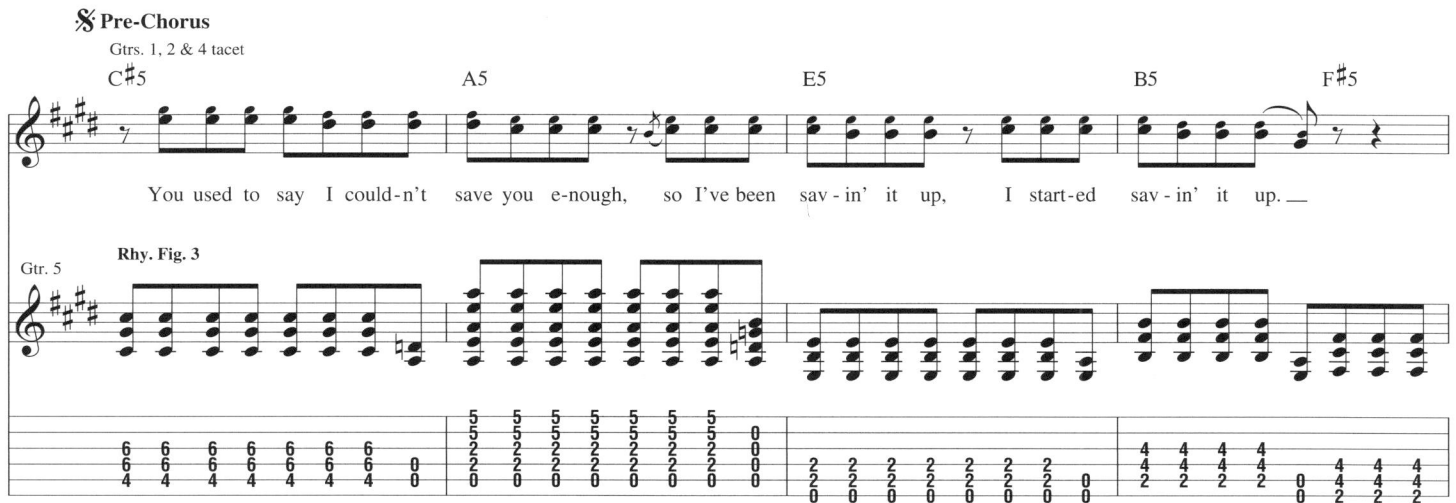

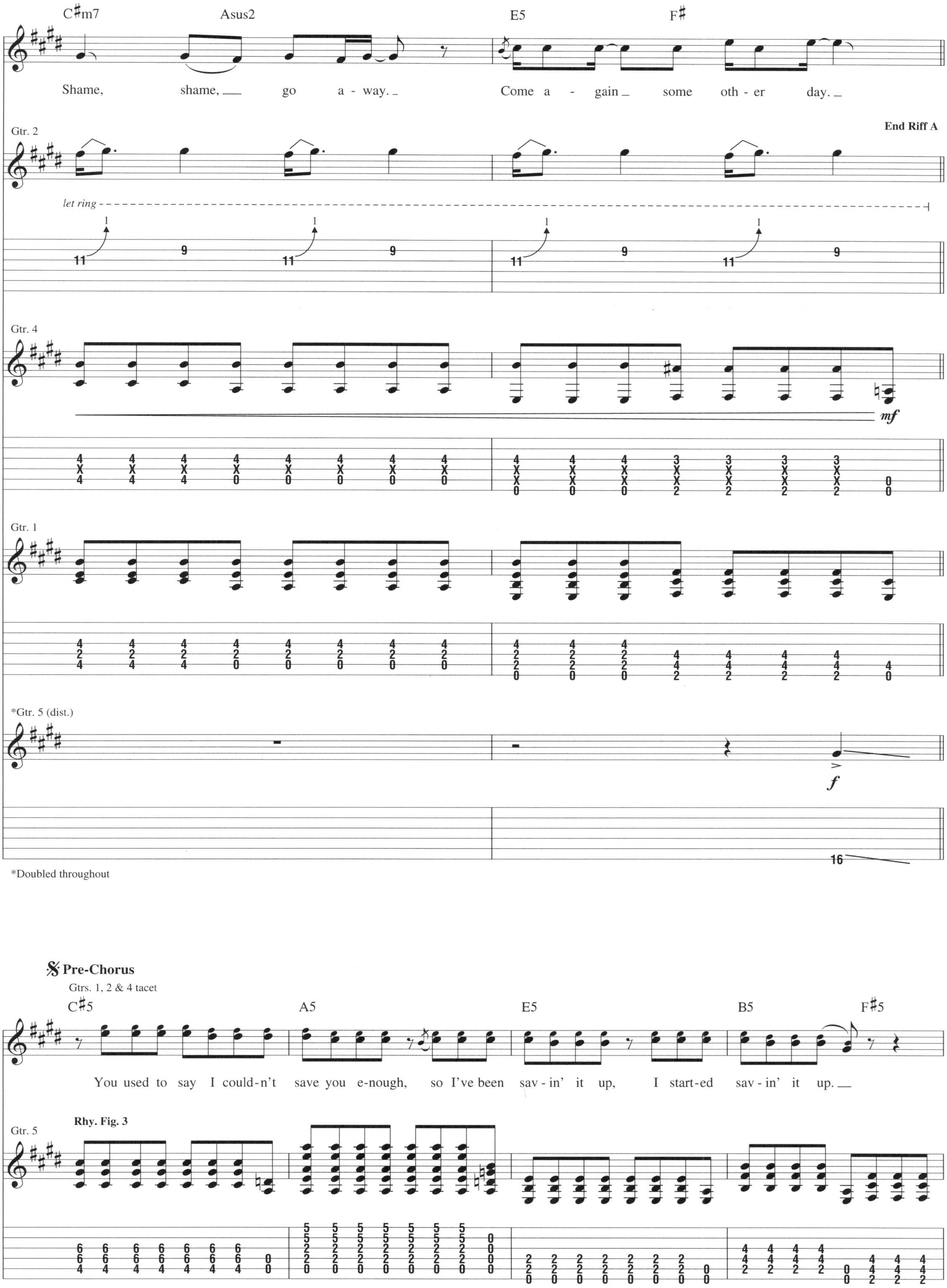

Aadd9
B5
C
Ar - lan - dri - a.
End Rhy. Fig. 4A
End Rhy. Fig. 4
End Rhy. Fig. 4B
Gtrs. 5, 6 & 7: w/ Rhy. Figs. 4, 4A & 4B
C♯m7
F♯7add4
You and what ar - my?
Ar - lan - dri - a,
To Coda
Aadd9
B5
C
Ar - lan - dri - a.
Oh, God, you got - ta make it

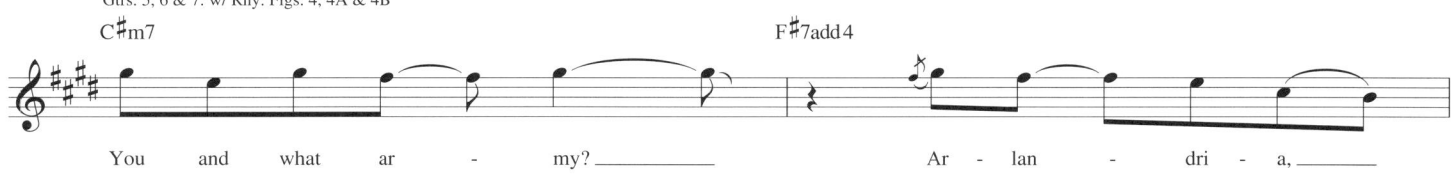

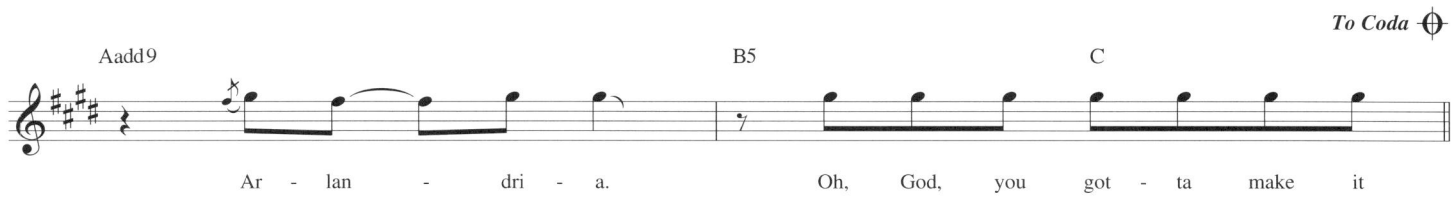

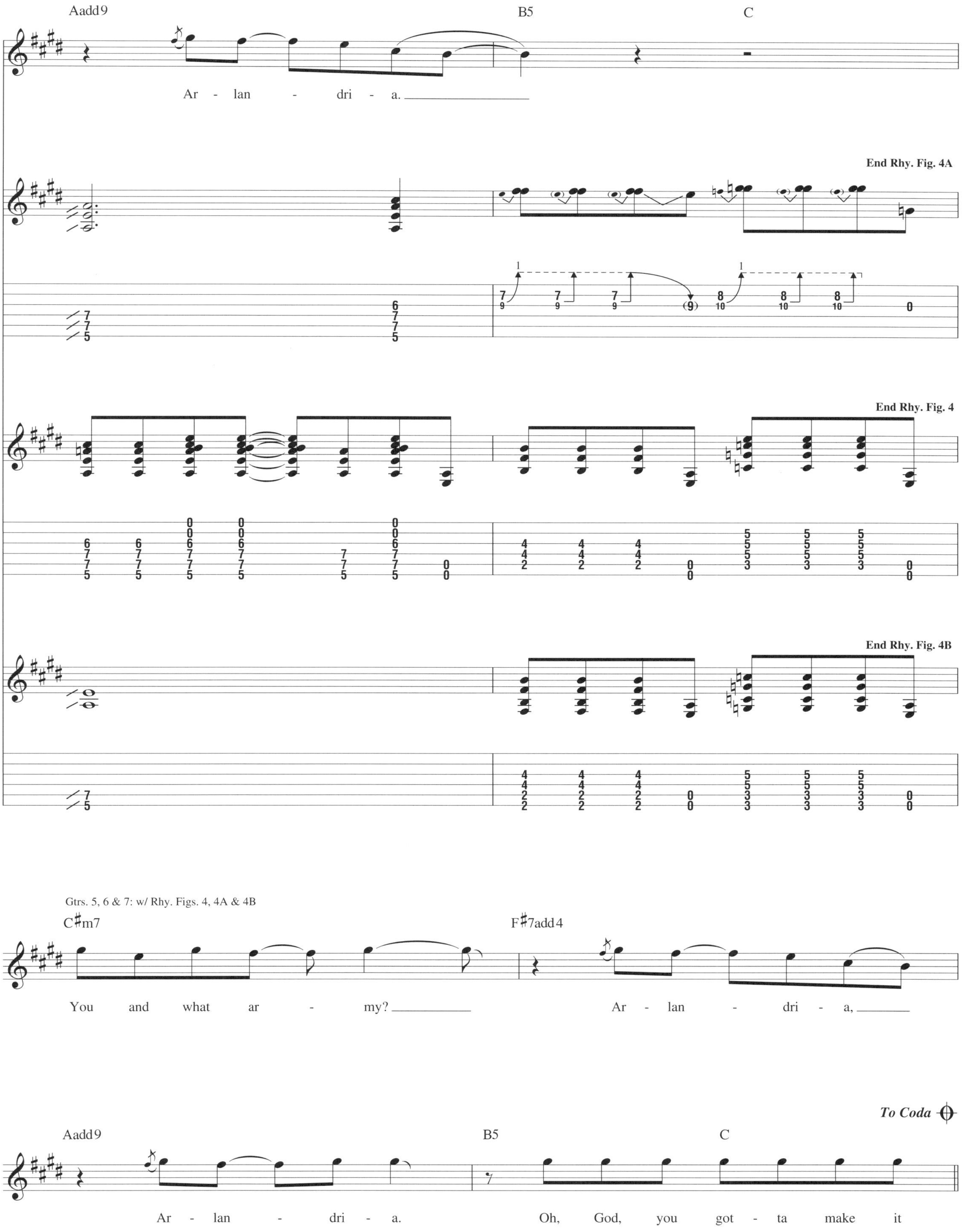

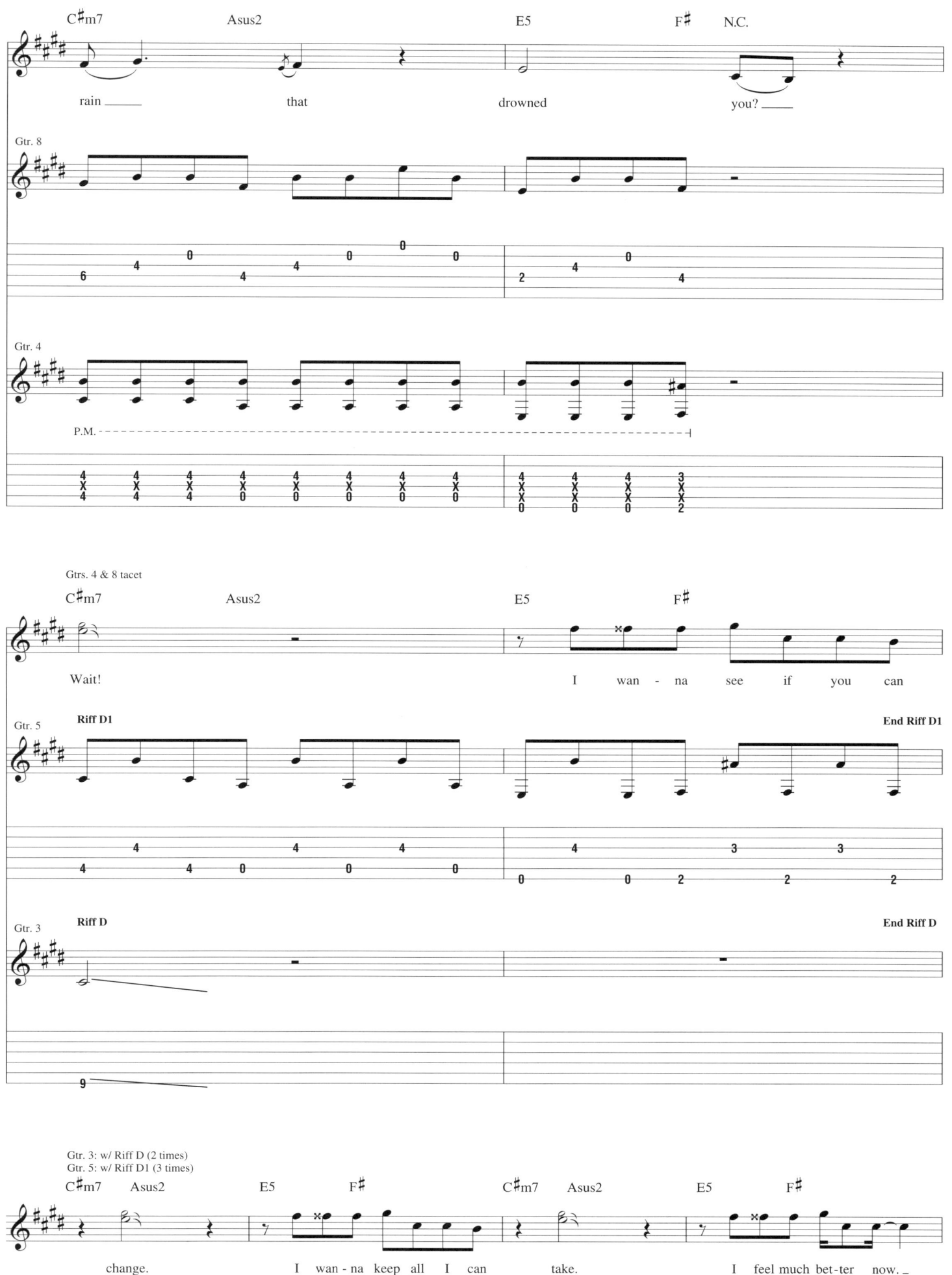

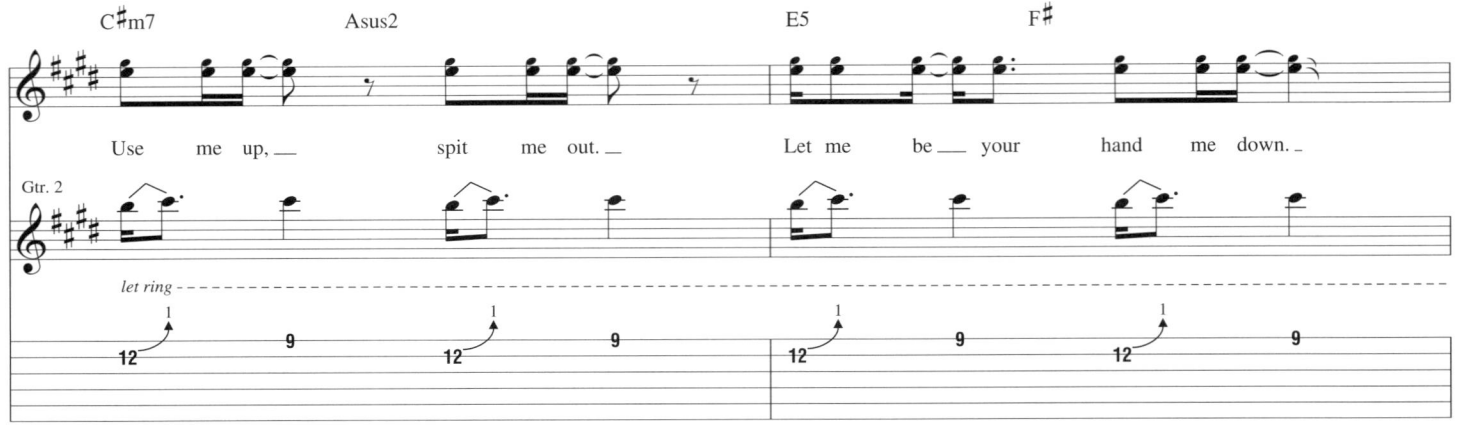

Coda

Bridge

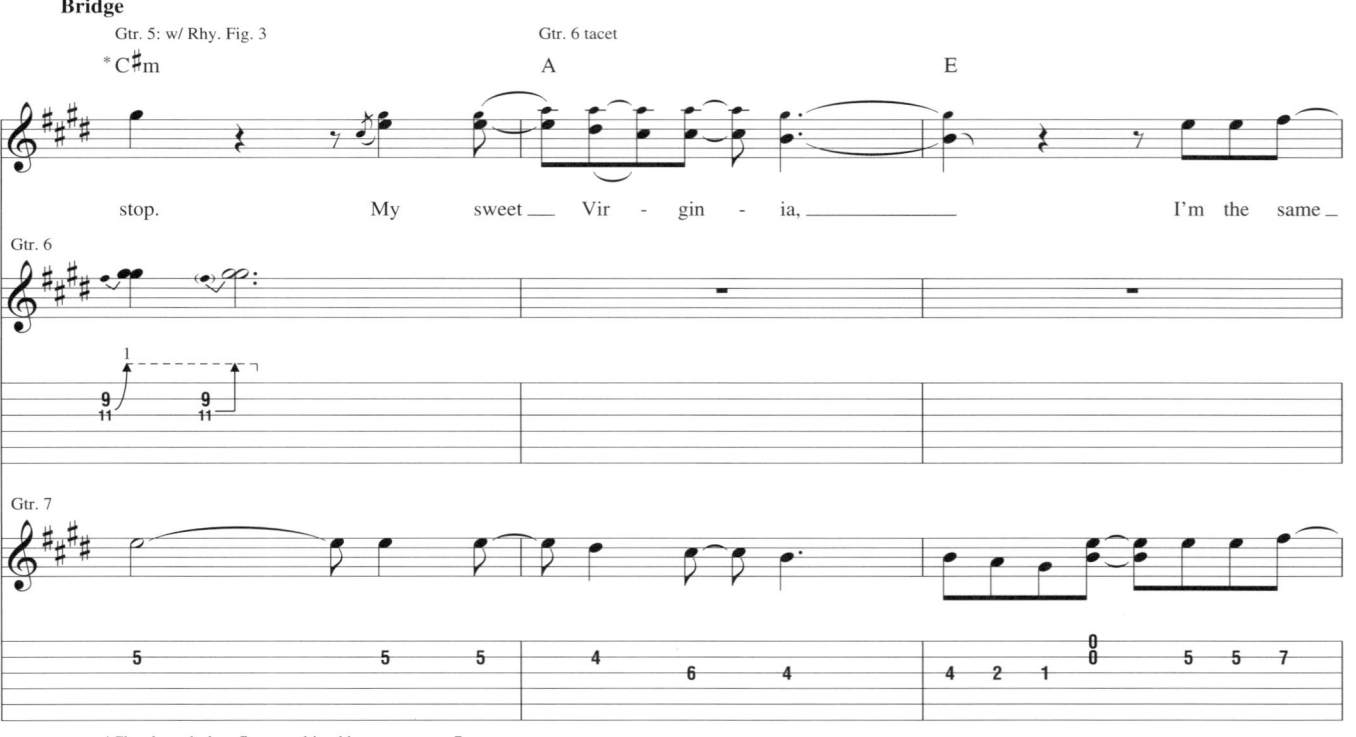

*Chord symbols reflect combined harmony, next 7 meas.

*Pluck strings behind nut.
**Set for quarter-note regeneration w/ multiple repeats (hold for next 12 meas.).

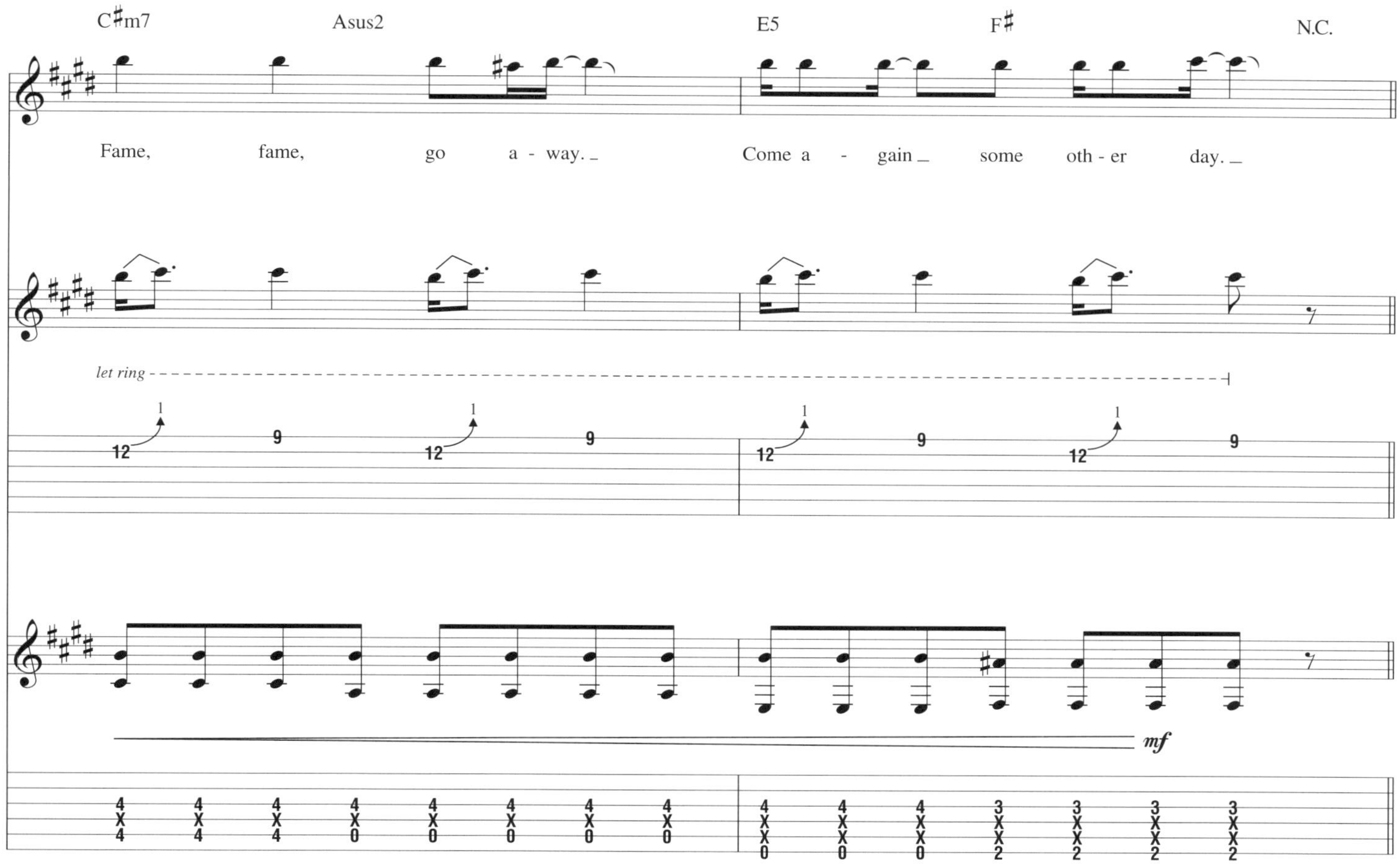
C♯m7
Asus2
E5
F♯
N.C.
Fame, fame, go a - way. _ Come a - gain _ some oth - er day. _
let ring
mf

Pre-Chorus

Gtrs. 2 & 4 tacet
Gtr. 5: w/ Rhy. Fig. 3

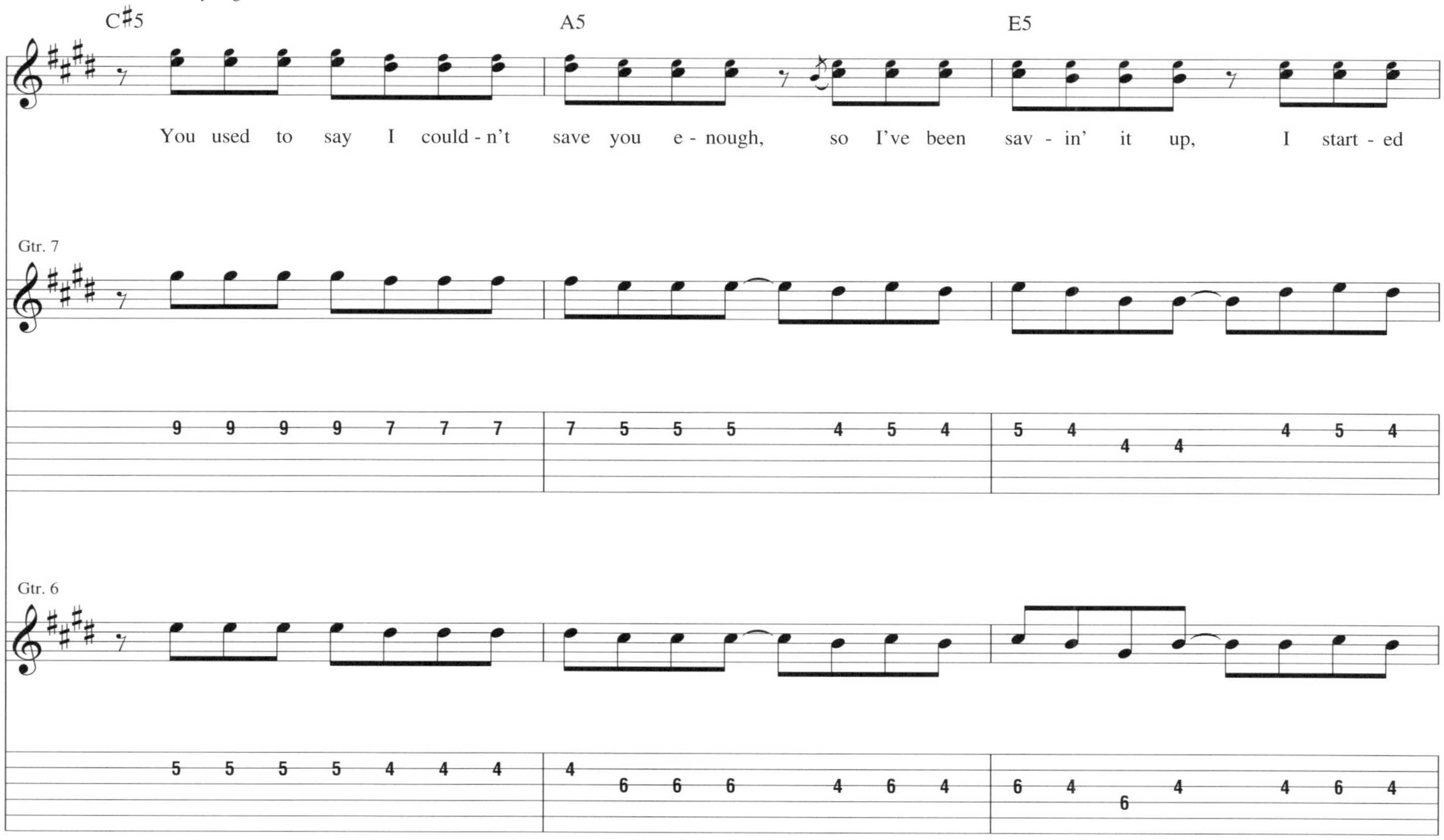
C♯5
A5
E5
You used to say I could - n't save you e - nough, so I've been sav - in' it up, I start - ed
Gtr. 7
Gtr. 6

These Days

Words and Music by David Grohl, Taylor Hawkins, Christopher Shiflett, Nate Mendel and Pat Smear

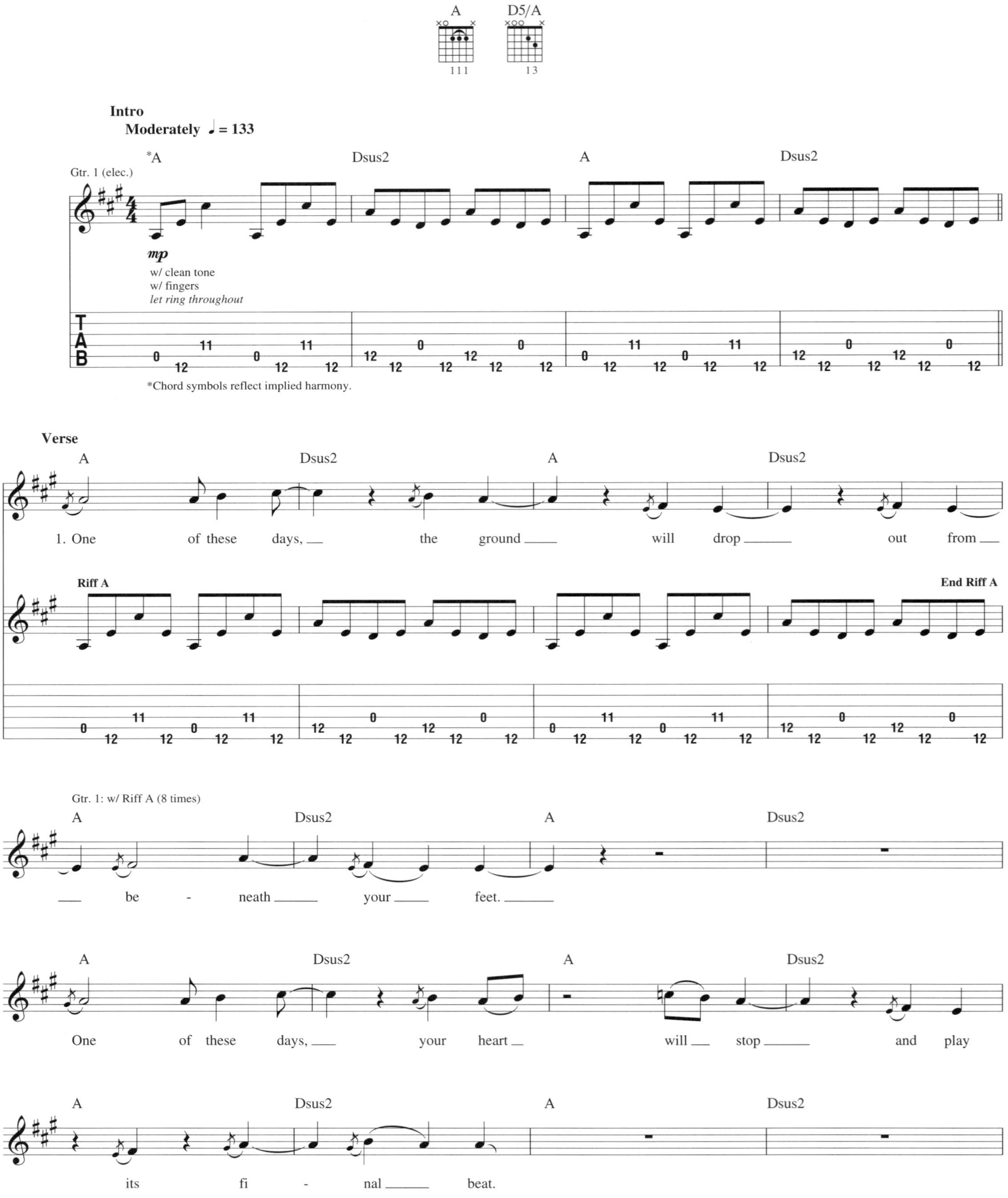

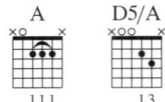

*Gtr. 5 (elec.) w/ dist.; Gtr. 6 (acous.).
Composite arrangement

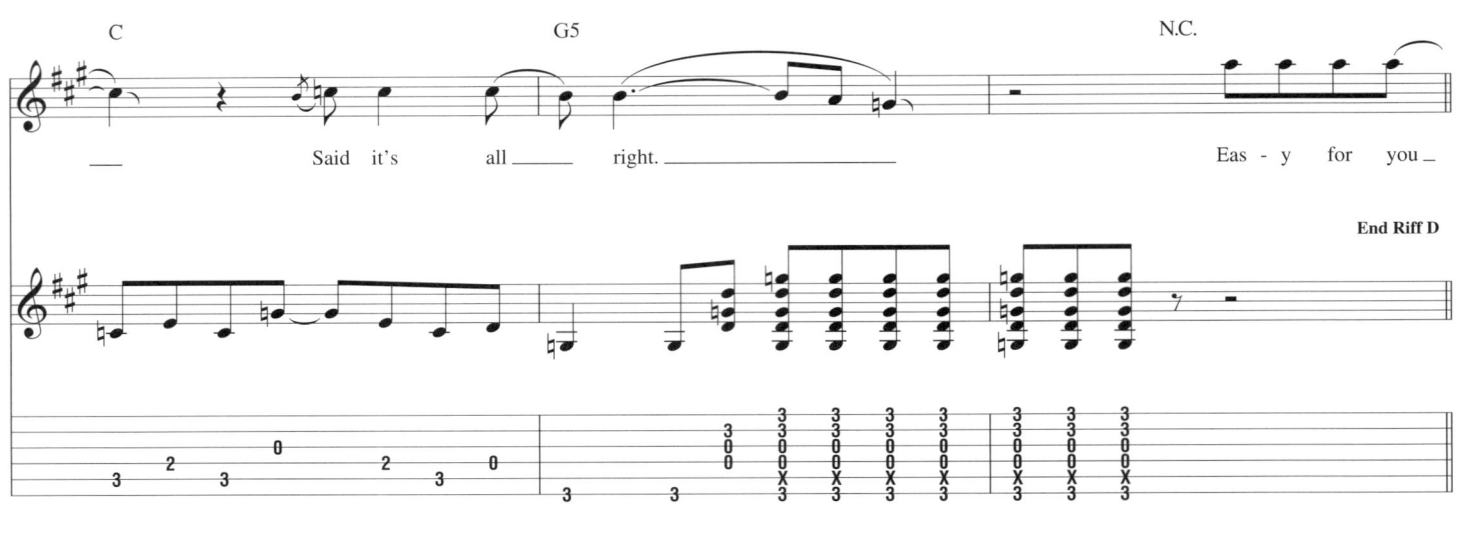

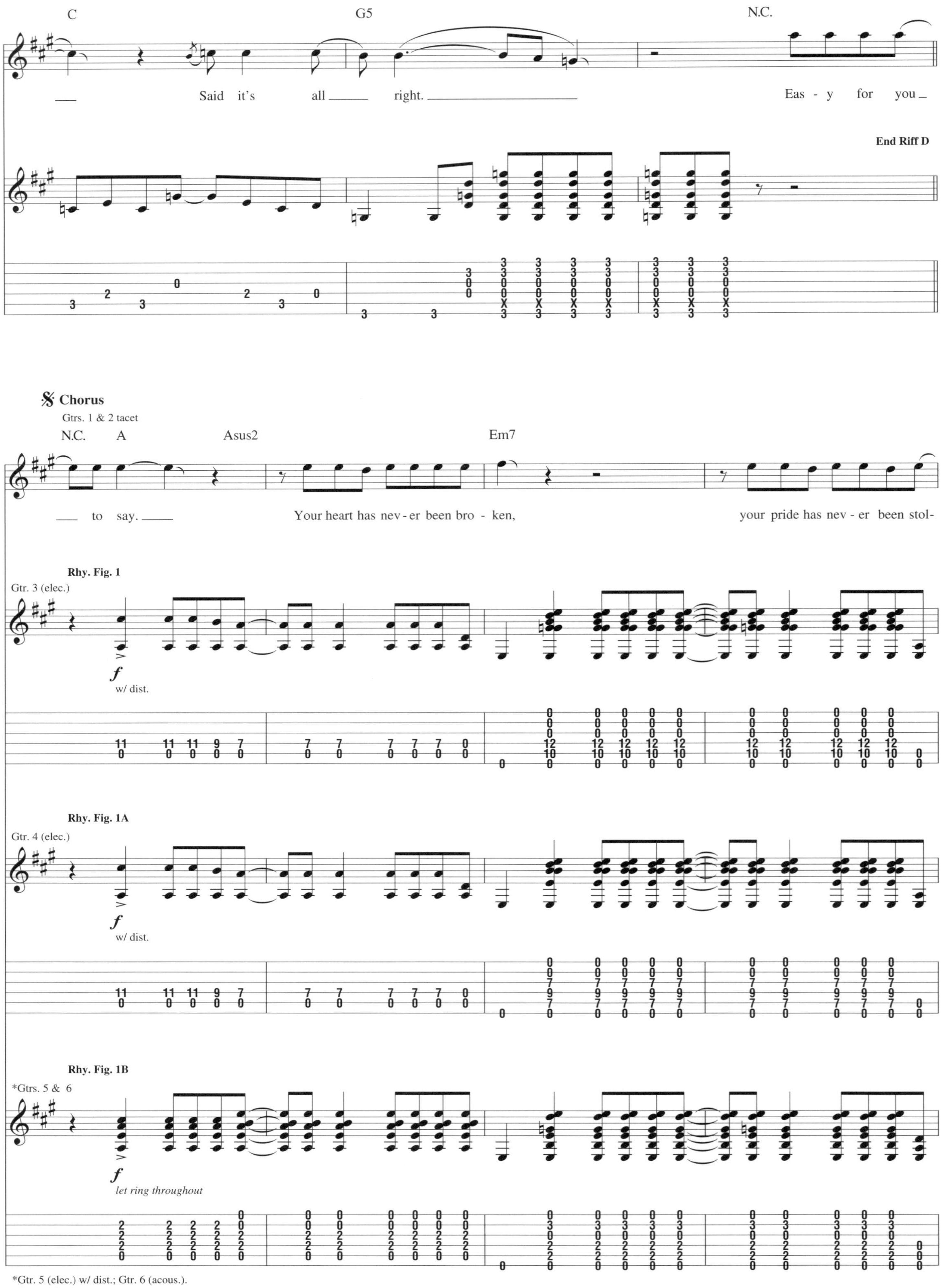

Cadd9
D
- en. Not yet, not yet. One of these
End Rhy. Fig. 1
End Rhy. Fig. 1A
End Rhy. Fig. 1B
Gtrs. 3 & 4: w/ Rhy. Figs. 1 & 1A
Gtrs. 5 & 6: w/ Rhy. Fig. 1B
N.C. A Asus2
Em7
days, I'll bet your heart-'ll be bro - ken. I'll bet your pride-'ll be stol -
Cadd9
D
- en. I bet, I bet, I bet, I bet. One of these

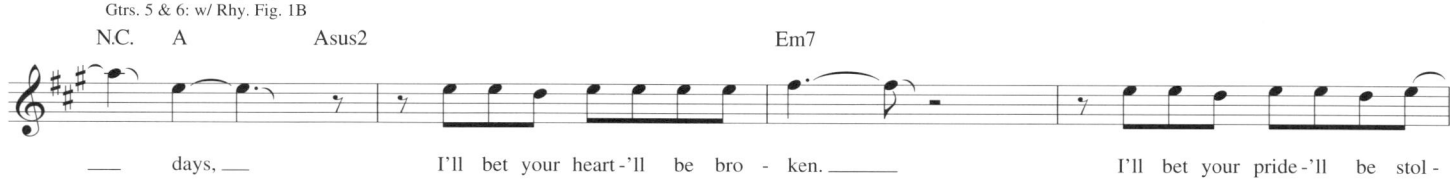

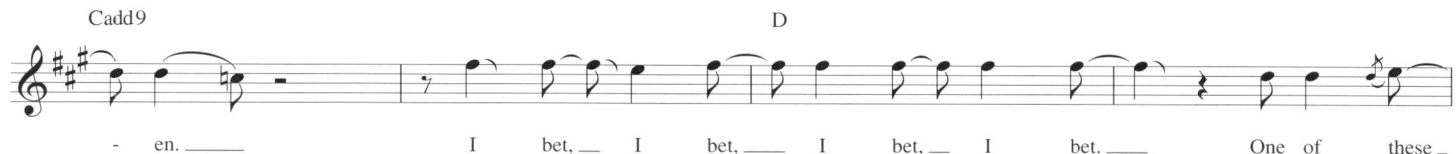

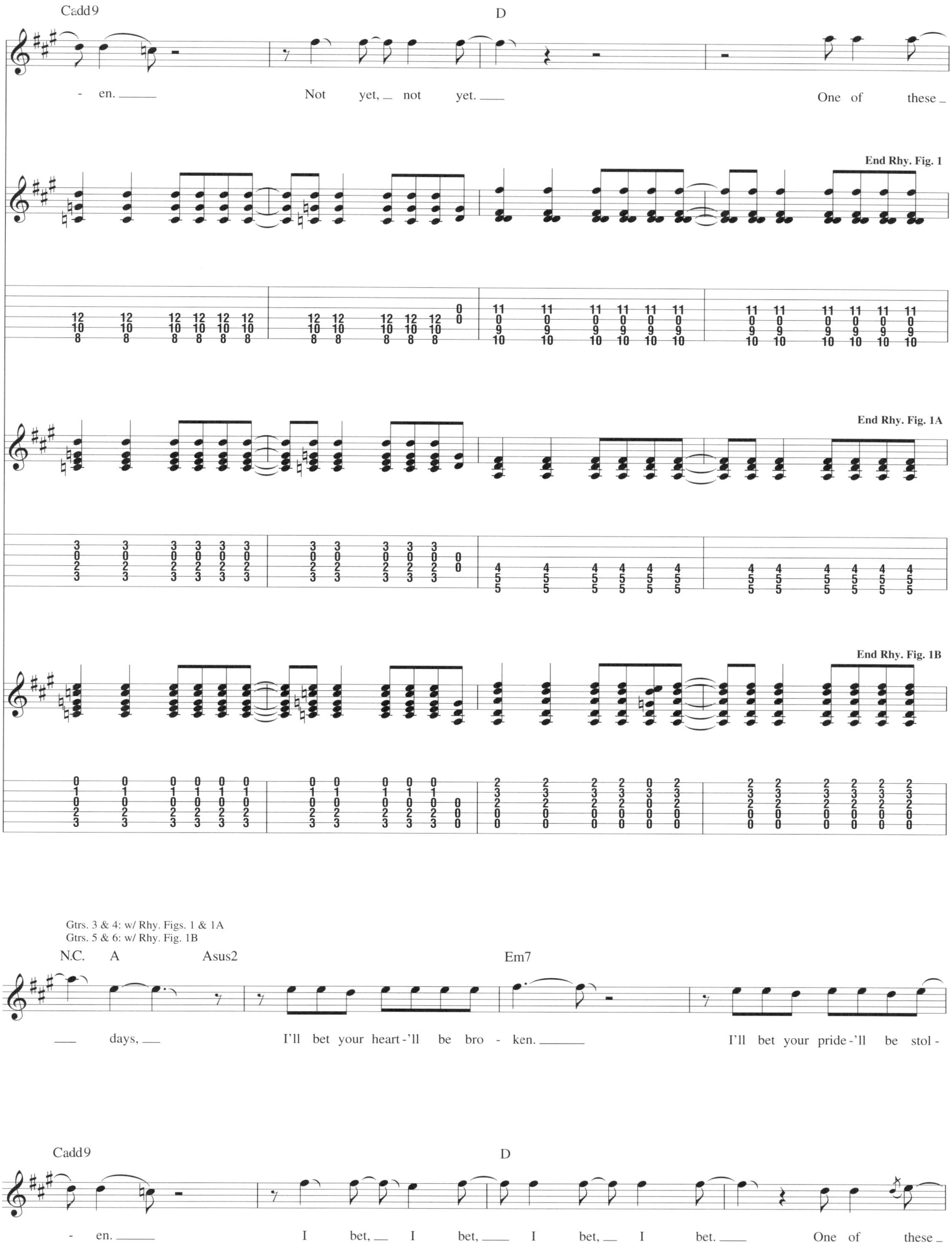

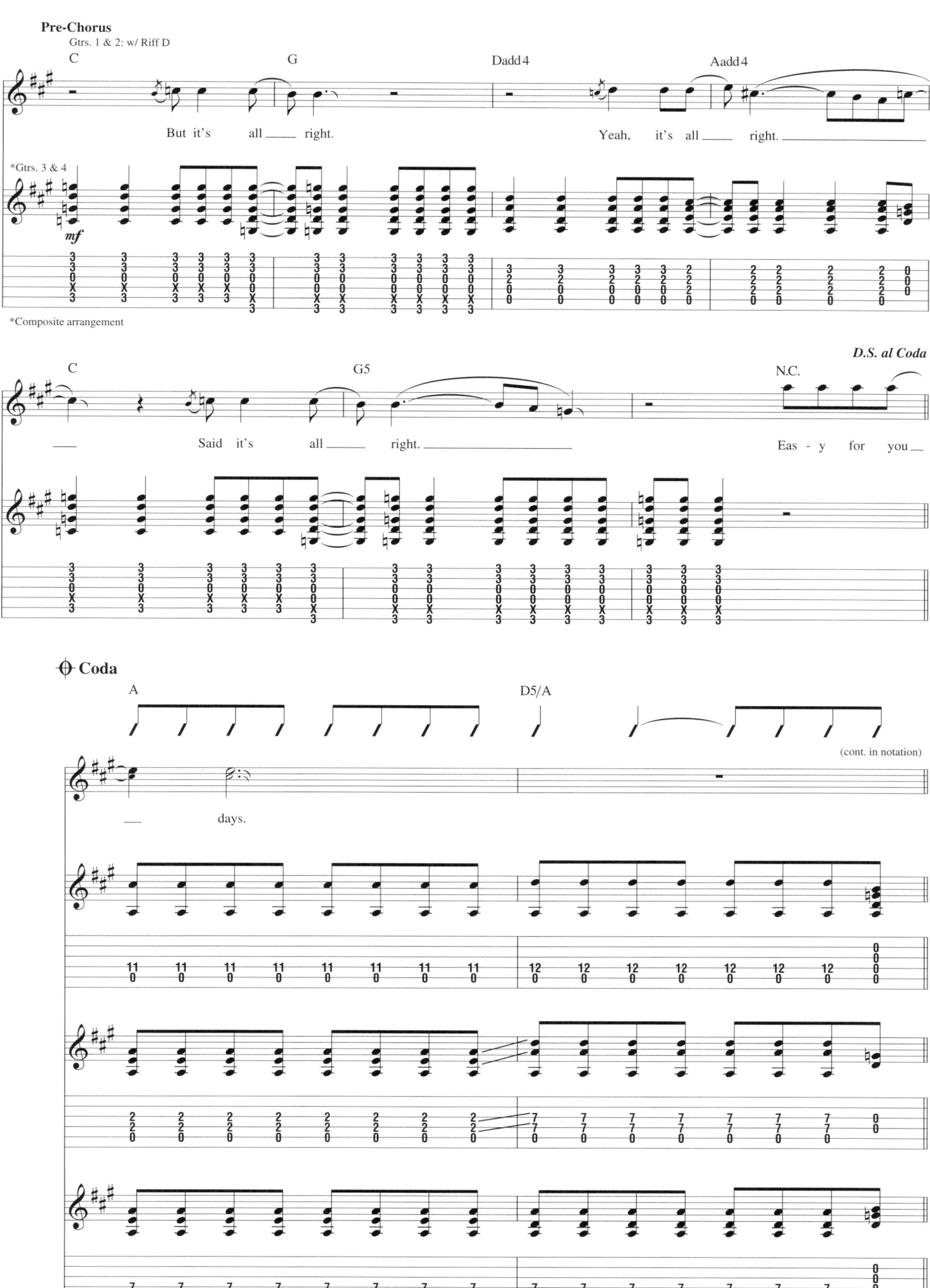

Back & Forth

Words and Music by David Grohl, Taylor Hawkins, Christopher Shiflett, Nate Mendel and Pat Smear

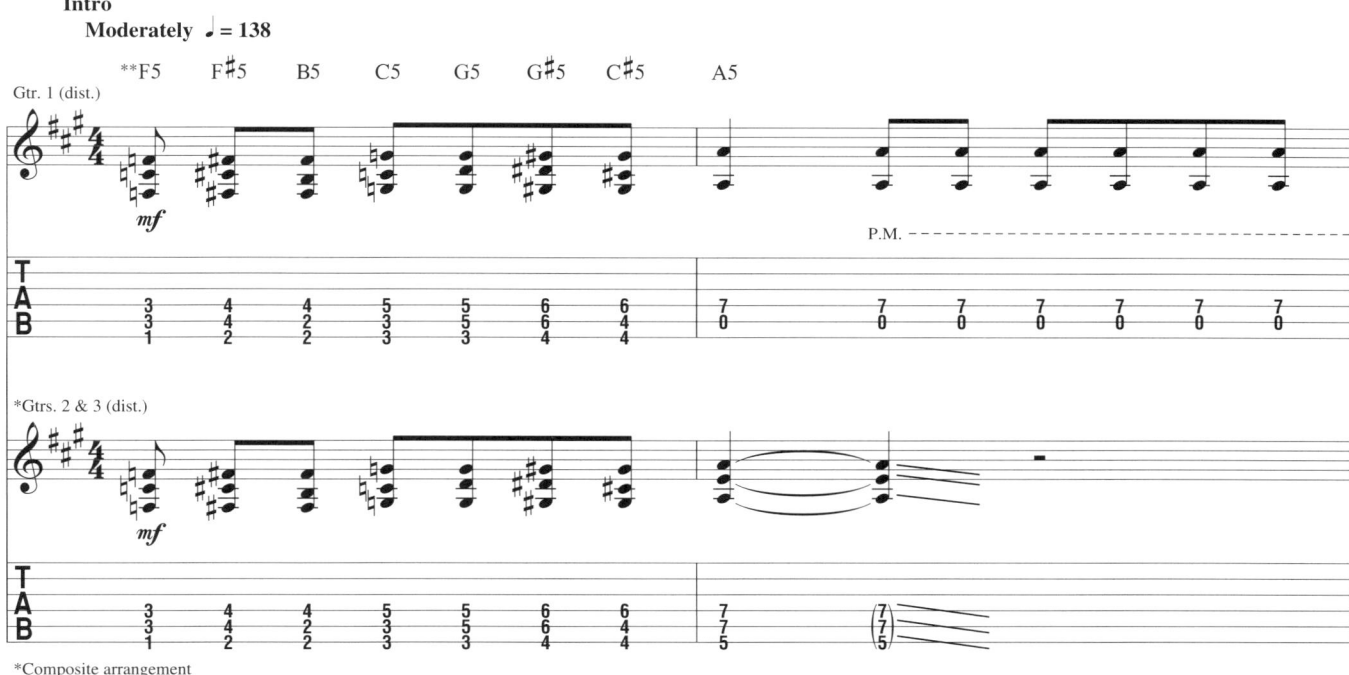

Verse
Gtr. 3 tacet
A5 Amaj7 A6 A5 C5 C(#4) C C(#4) G
you're on your own, worn through the pag - es. O - ver the hill and through the ag - es. Does
Rhy. Fig. 2
*Gtrs. 1 & 2
End Rhy. Fig. 2
P.M.
*Composite arrangement
Rhy. Fill 1
End Rhy. Fill 1
Gtr. 3
Gsus4 G5 G6 D Dsus4 D5 N.C. F5 F#5 B5 C5 G5 G#5 C#5
Gtr. 3: w/ Rhy. Fig. 1 (last meas.)
my heav - en burn like hell on you? Half
Gtrs. 1 & 2
P.M.
Gtrs. 1 & 2: w/ Rhy. Fig. 2
Gtr. 3: w/ Rhy. Fill 1
A5 Amaj7 A6 A5 C5 C(#4) C C(#4) G
be-neath the cracks, they're com-ing in waves. Roll - ing like an earth-quake un-der the pave - ment. Where

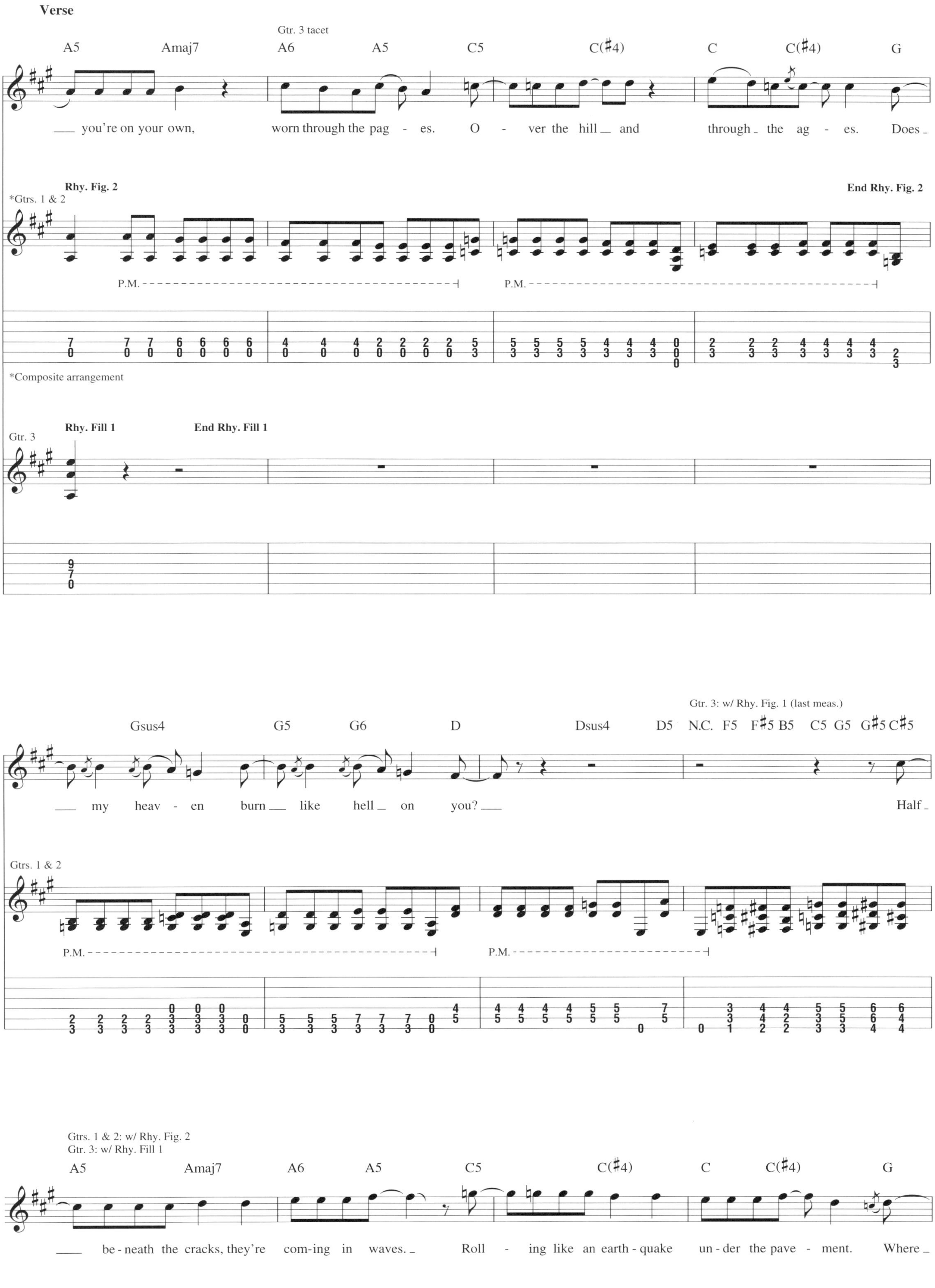

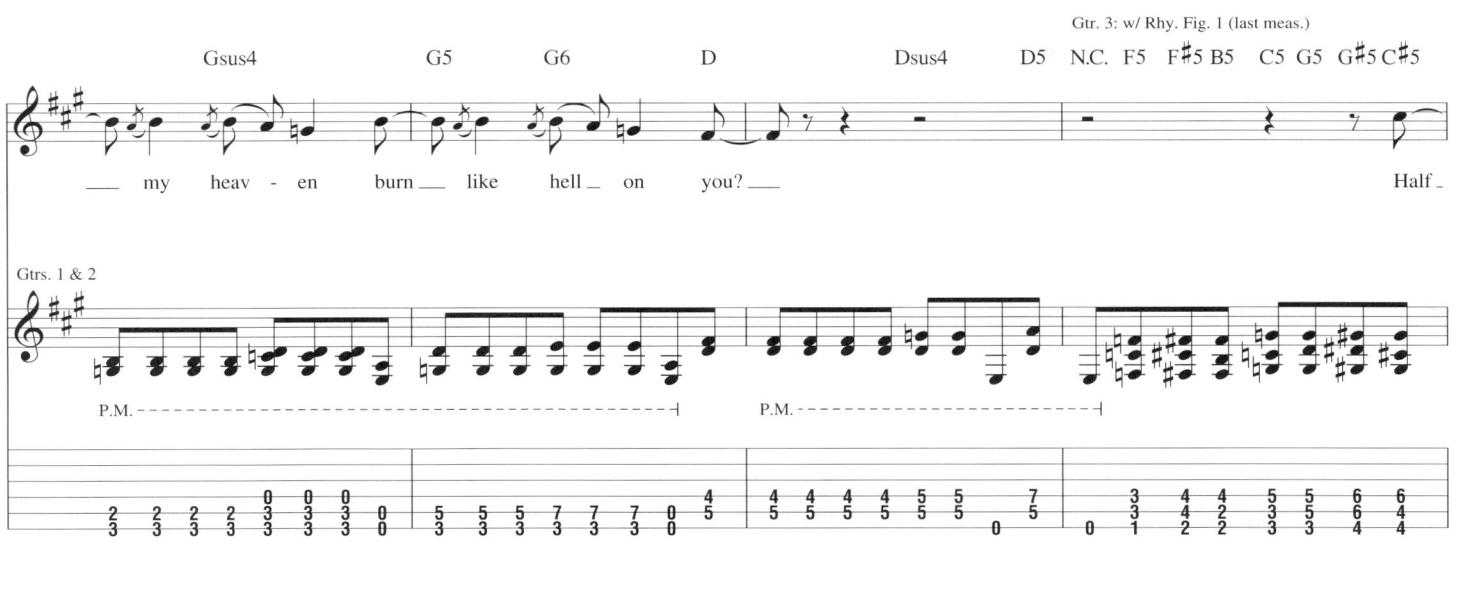

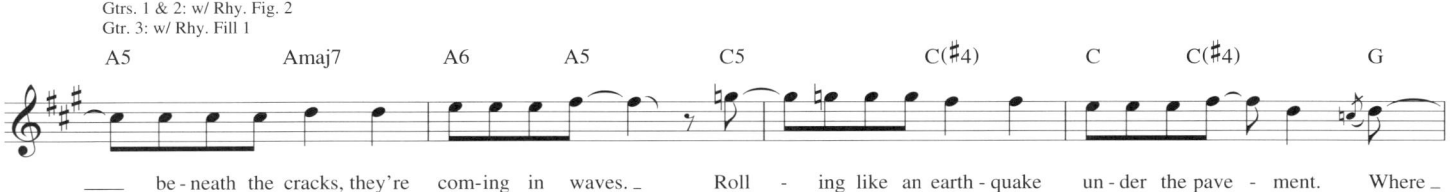

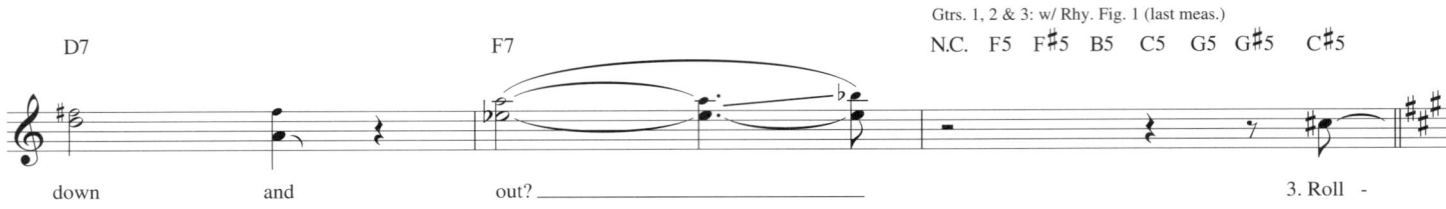

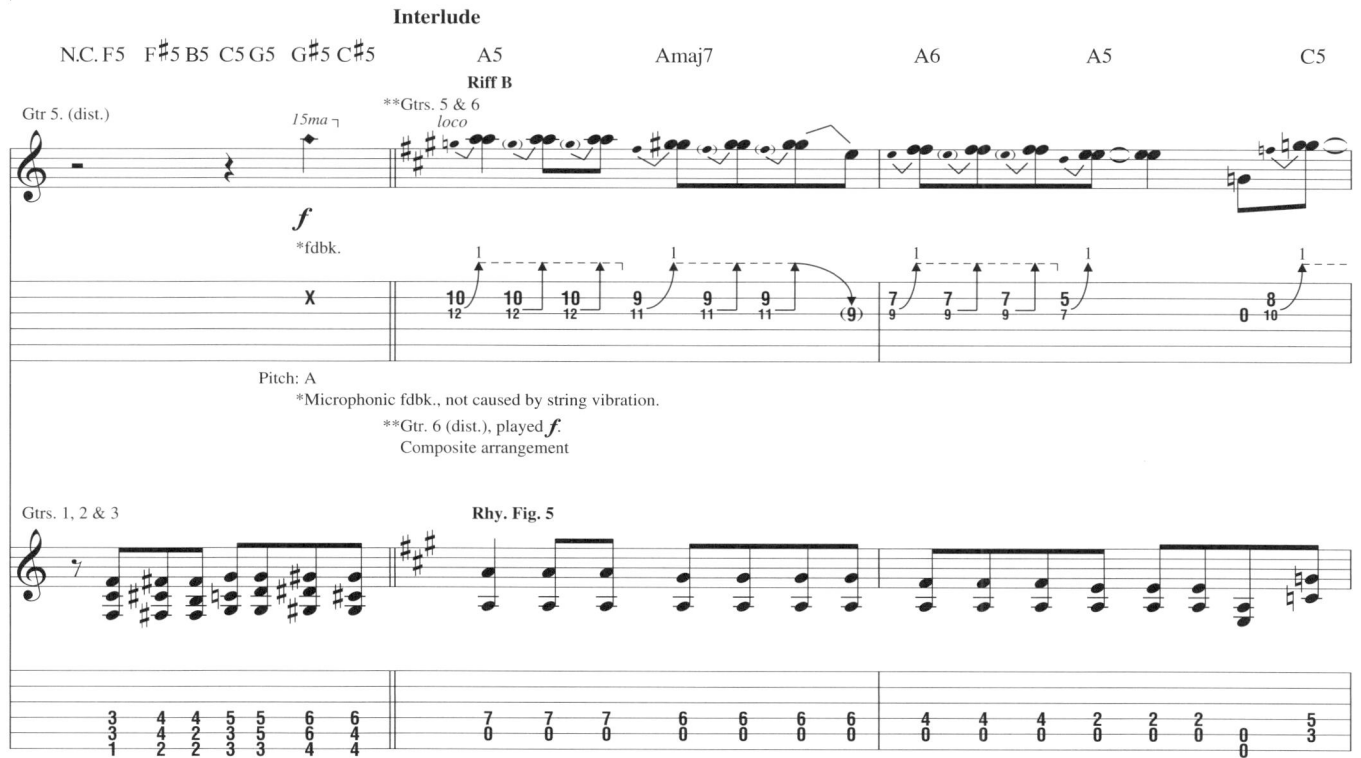

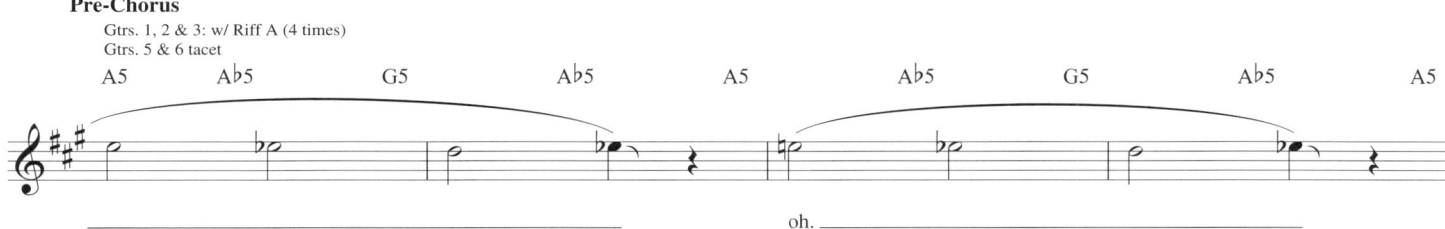

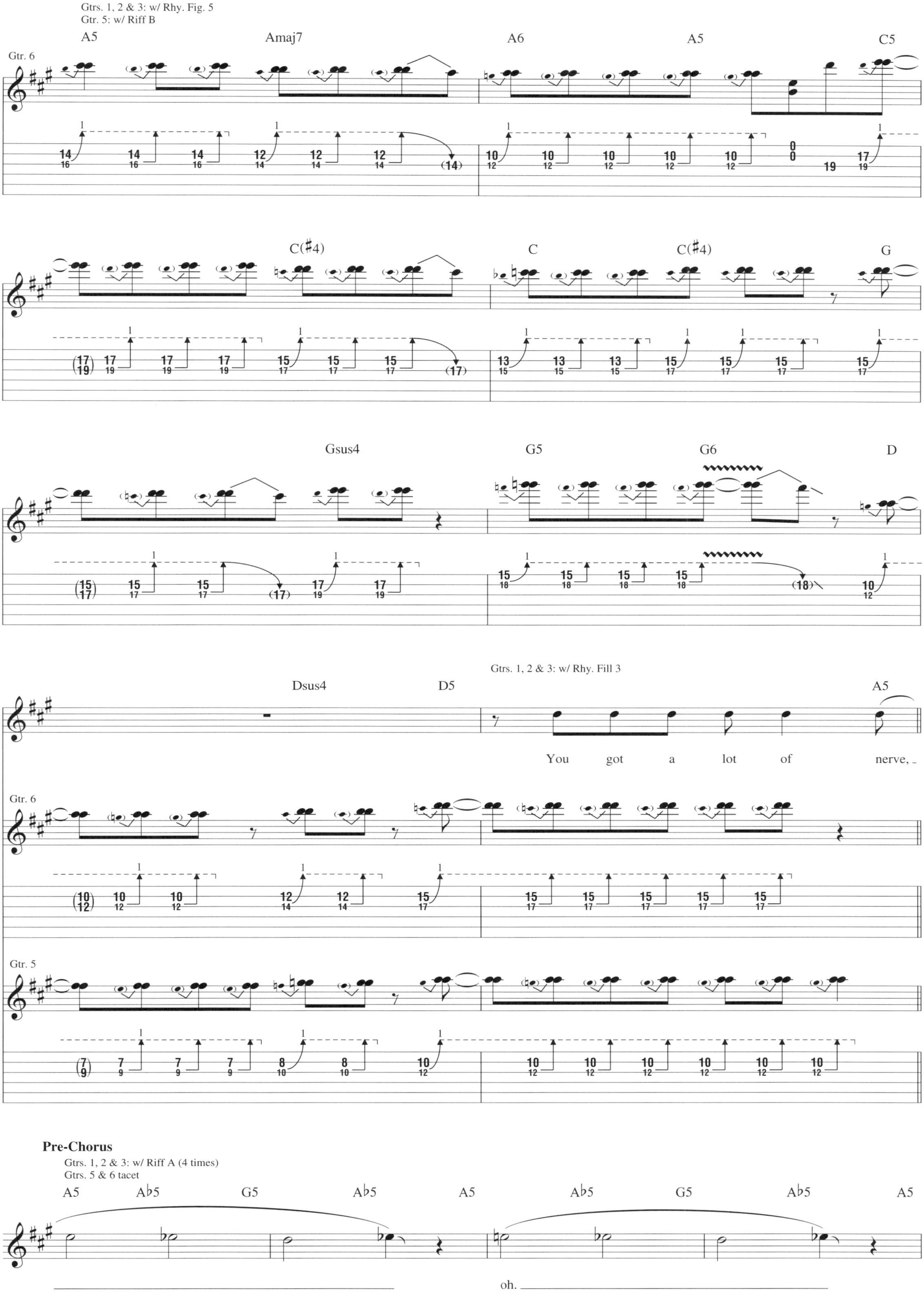
Gtrs. 1, 2 & 3: w/ Rhy. Fig. 5
Gtr. 5: w/ Riff B
A5
Amaj7
A6
A5
C5
Gtr. 6
C(♯4)
C
C(♯4)
G
Gsus4
G5
G6
D
Gtrs. 1, 2 & 3: w/ Rhy. Fill 3
Dsus4
D5
A5
You got a lot of nerve,
Gtr. 6
Gtr. 5
Pre-Chorus
Gtrs. 1, 2 & 3: w/ Riff A (4 times)
Gtrs. 5 & 6 tacet
A5
A♭5
G5
A♭5
A5
A♭5
G5
A♭5
A5
oh.

A Matter of Time

Words and Music by David Grohl, Taylor Hawkins, Christopher Shiflett, Nate Mendel and Pat Smear

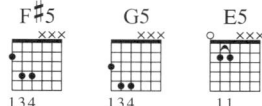

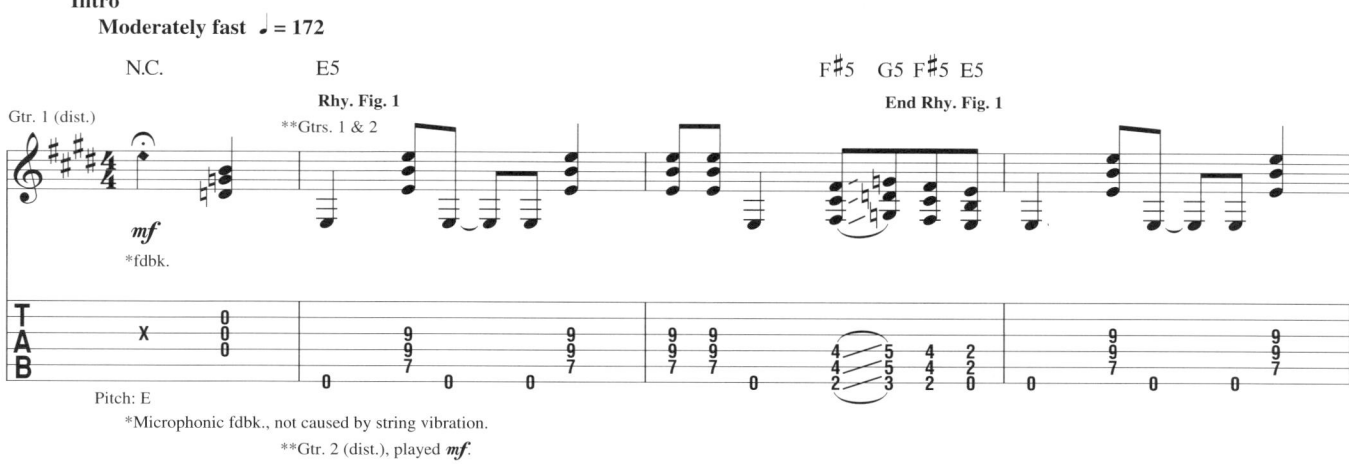

Copyright © 2011 SONGS OF UNIVERSAL, INC., MJ TWELVE MUSIC, LIVING UNDER A ROCK MUSIC,
I LOVE THE PUNK ROCK MUSIC, FLYING EARFORM MUSIC and RUTHENSMEAR MUSIC
All Rights for MJ TWELVE MUSIC and I LOVE THE PUNK ROCK MUSIC Controlled and Administered by SONGS OF UNIVERSAL, INC.
All Rights for LIVING UNDER A ROCK MUSIC Controlled and Administered by UNIVERSAL MUSIC CORP.
All Rights for FLYING EARFORM MUSIC and RUTHENSMEAR MUSIC Administered by BUG MUSIC
All Rights Reserved   Used by Permission

Gtrs. 2 & 3: w/ Riffs A & A1
Aadd9
Am6/9
need an ar - my to sum - mon
Eadd9
Pre-Chorus
Am(add9)
me.
It does - n't mat-ter much to me
Gtr. 1
Rhy. Fill 2
End Rhy. Fill 2
Gtr. 2
Rhy. Fill 2A
End Rhy. Fill 2A
let ring
Eadd9
if it does - n't mat-ter much to you,

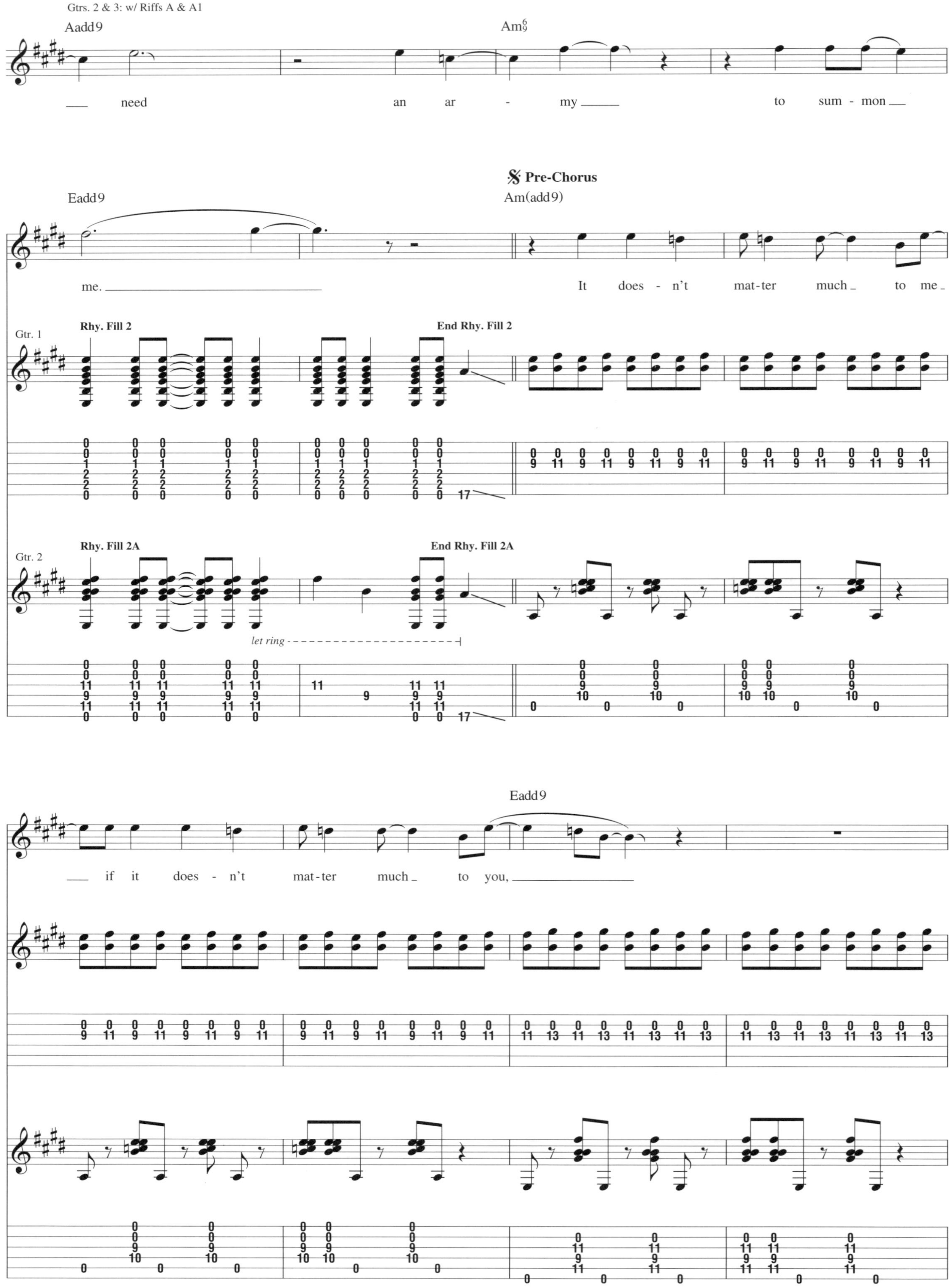

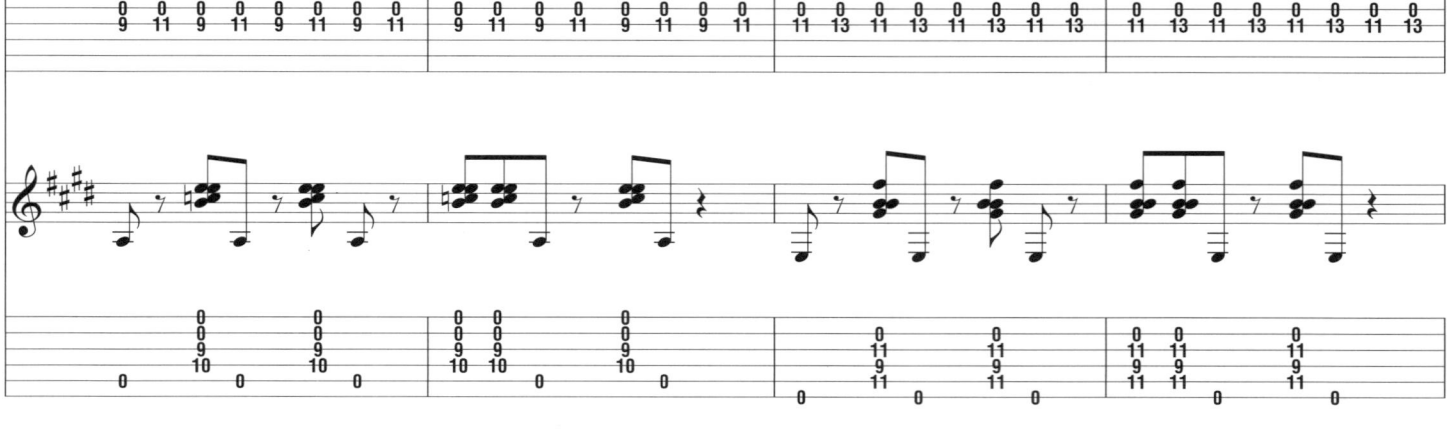

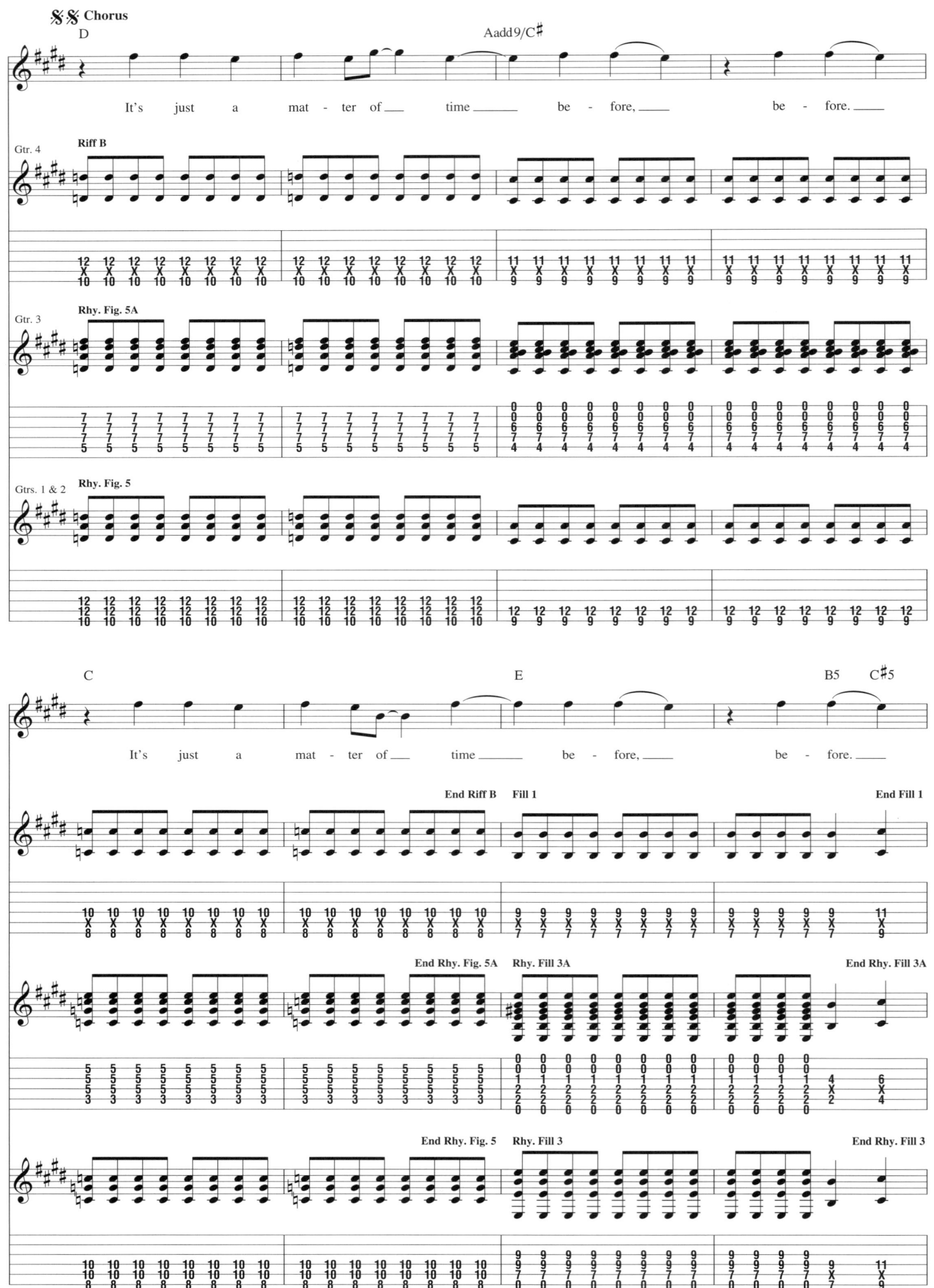

Bridge
Gtrs. 3 & 4 tacet
Am(add9)
Where the hell were
Gtr. 1
Gtr. 2
Eadd9
you?
Oo.

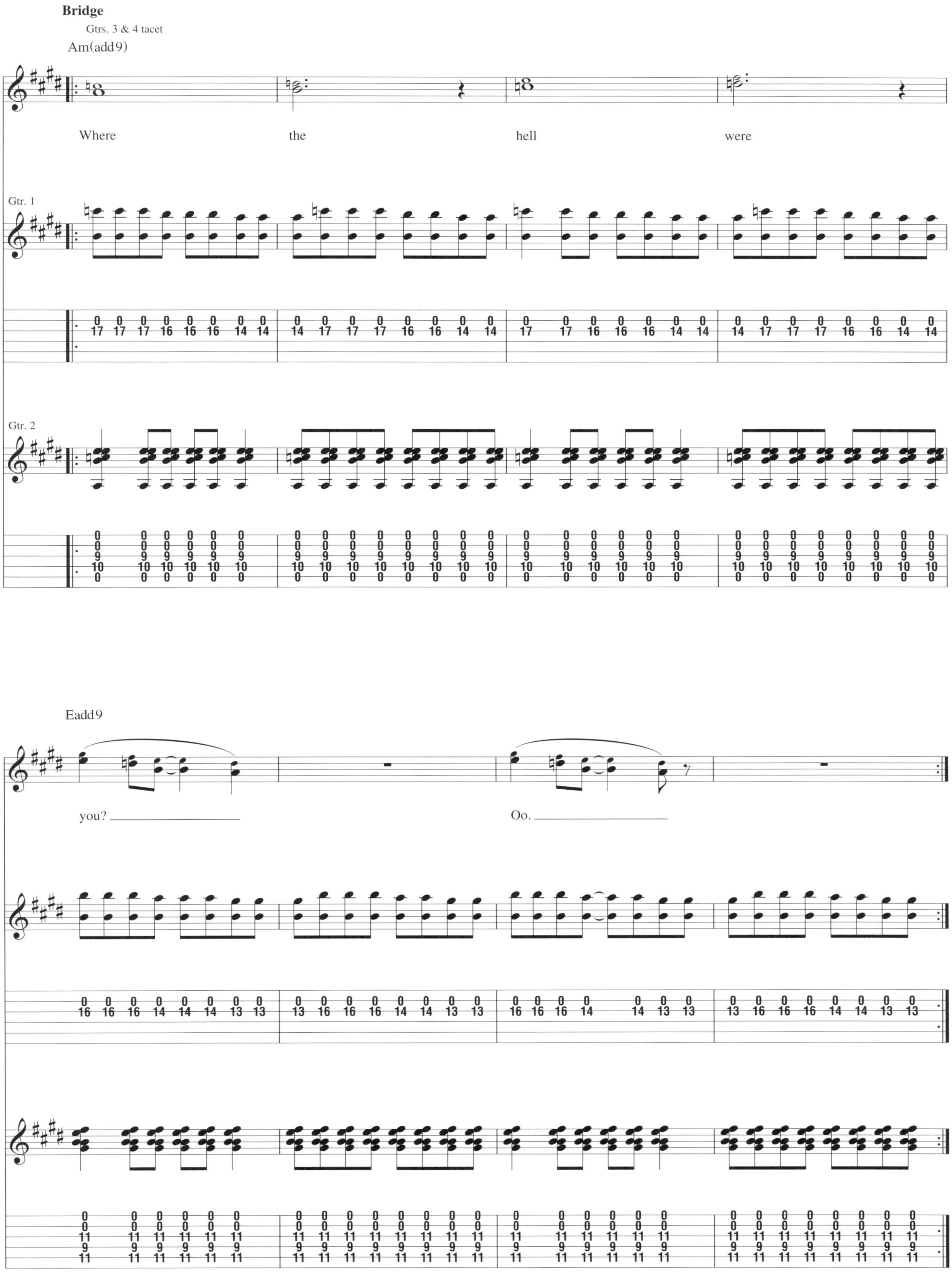

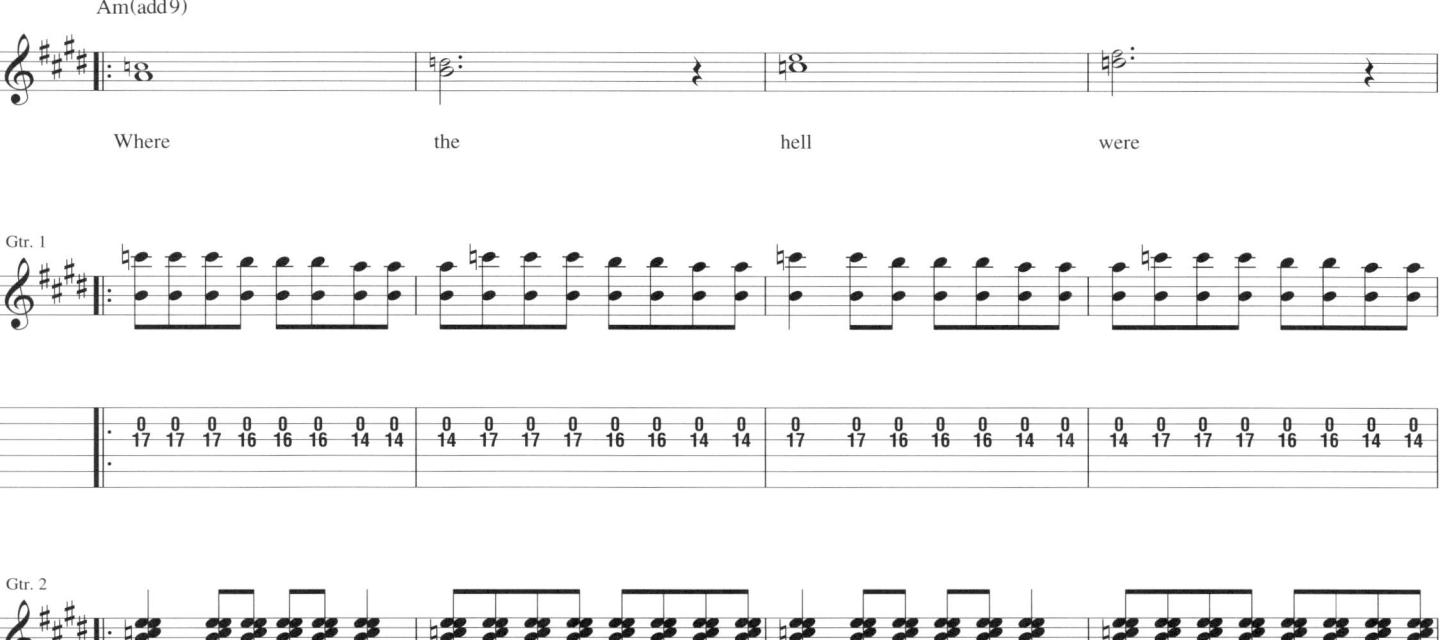

Am(add9)
Where the hell were
Gtr. 1
Gtr. 3
Fill 2
End Fill 2
Gtr. 2
D.S.S. al Coda 2
Gtrs. 1, 2 & 3: w/ Rhy. Fig. 1
E5
F♯5 G5 F♯5 E5
Gtrs. 1, 2 & 3: w/ Rhy. Fig. 2
B5 C♯5
you?
Gtr. 4

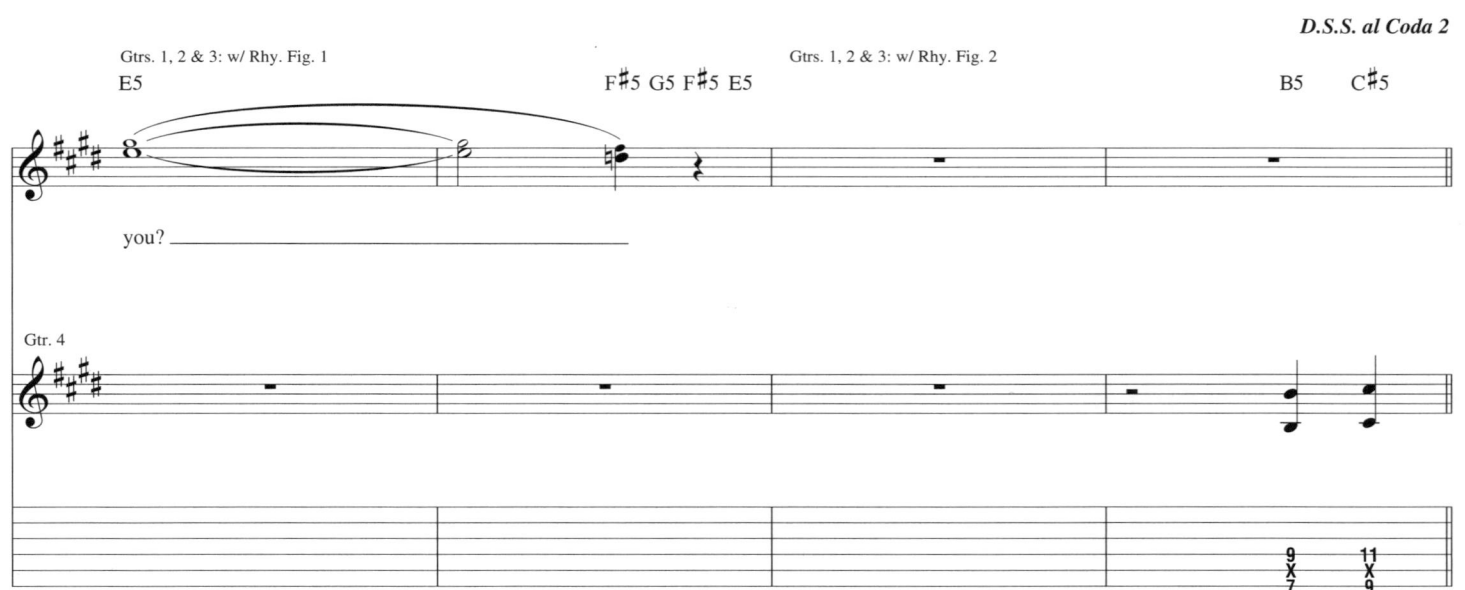

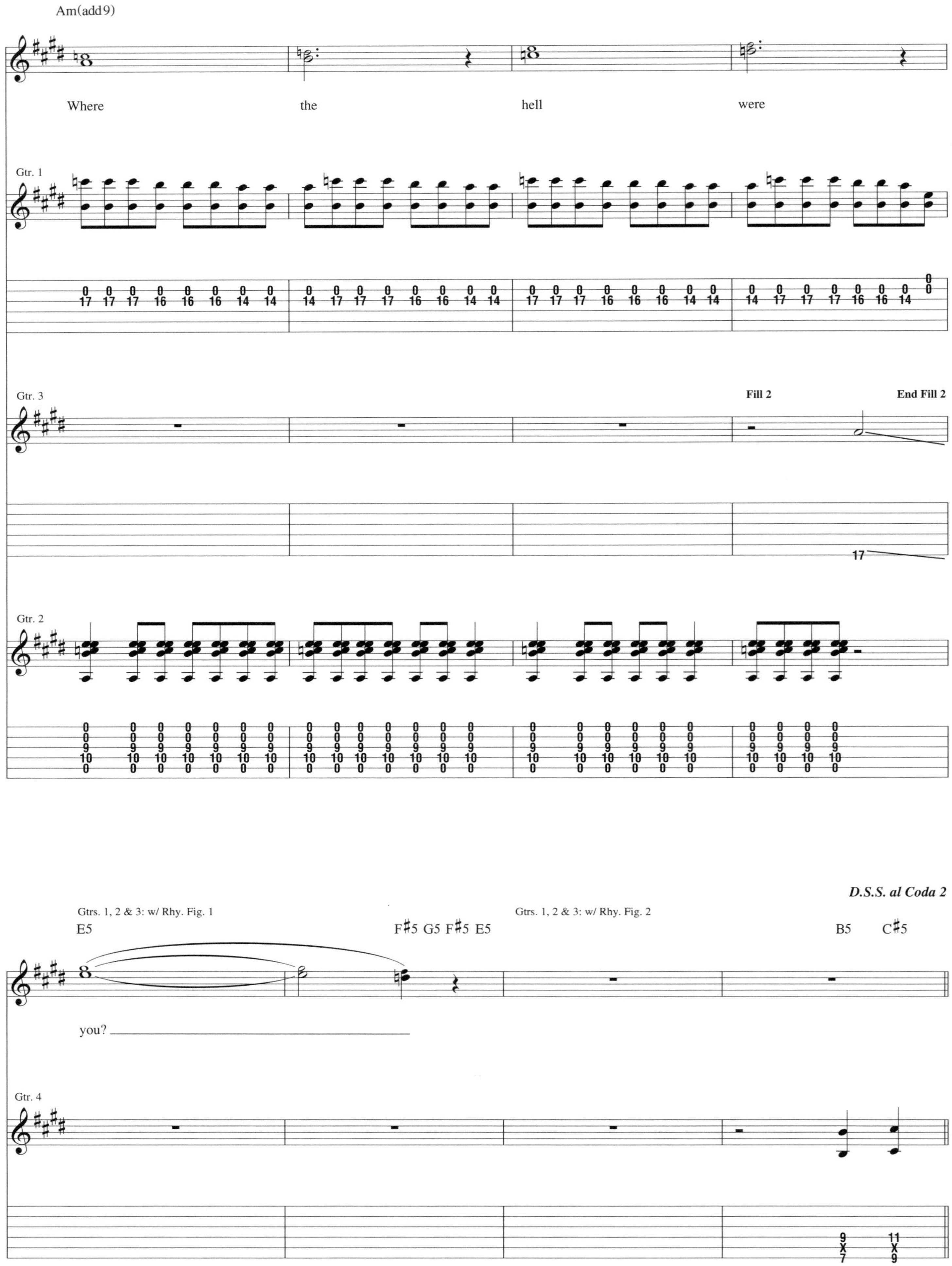

Coda 2

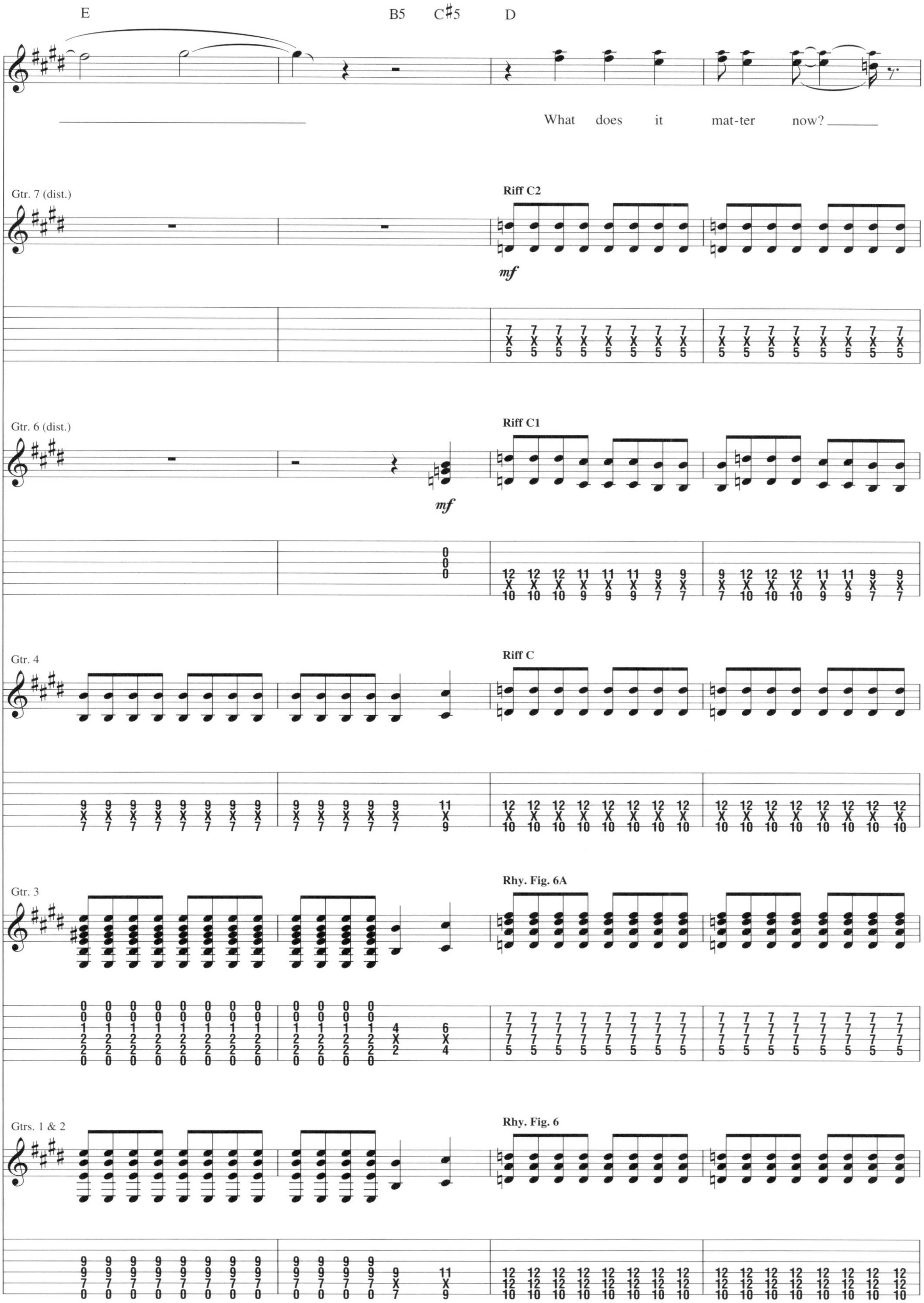
E
B5
C♯5
D
What does it mat-ter now?
Gtr. 7 (dist.)
Riff C2
mf
Gtr. 6 (dist.)
Riff C1
mf
Gtr. 4
Riff C
Gtr. 3
Rhy. Fig. 6A
Gtrs. 1 & 2
Rhy. Fig. 6

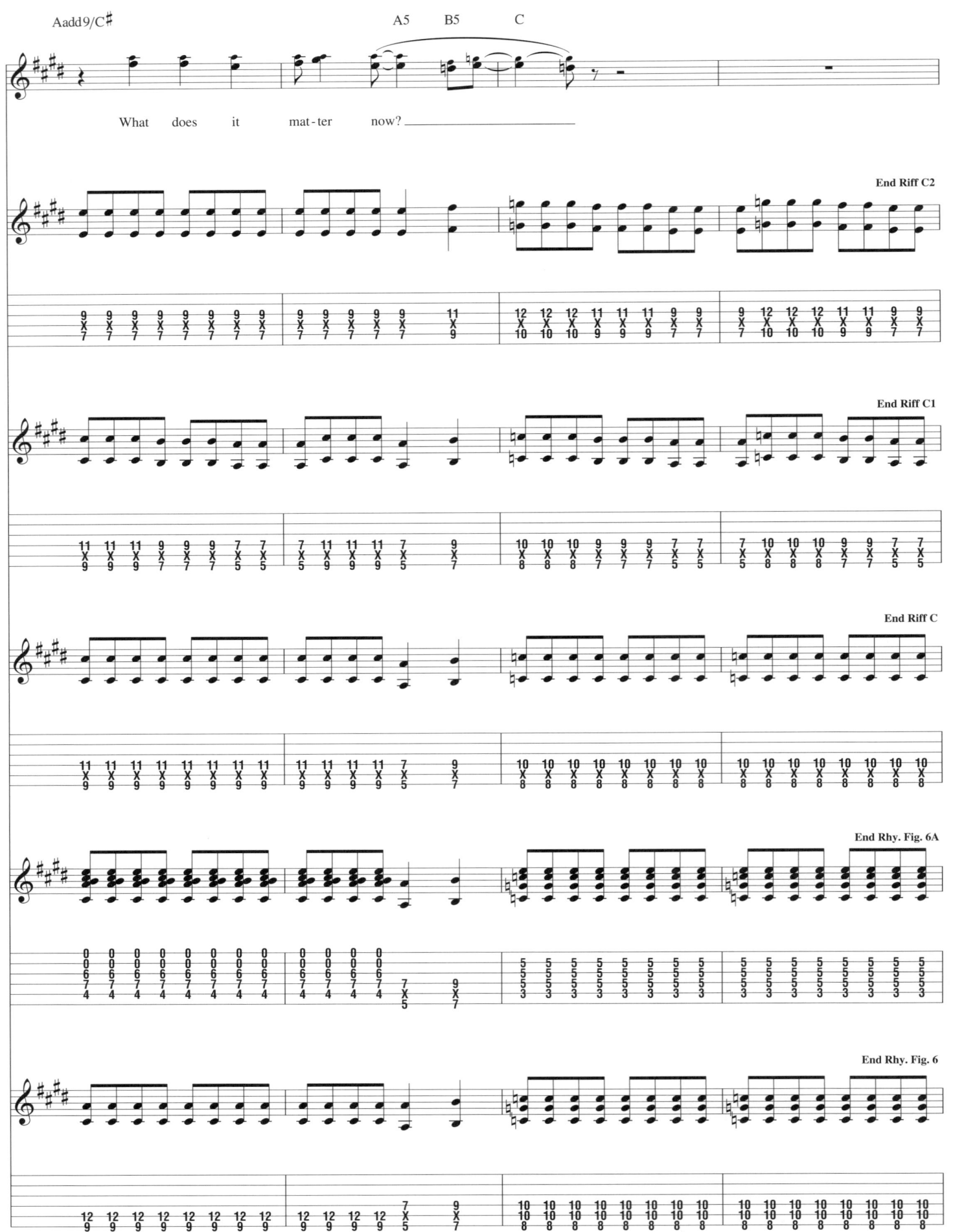

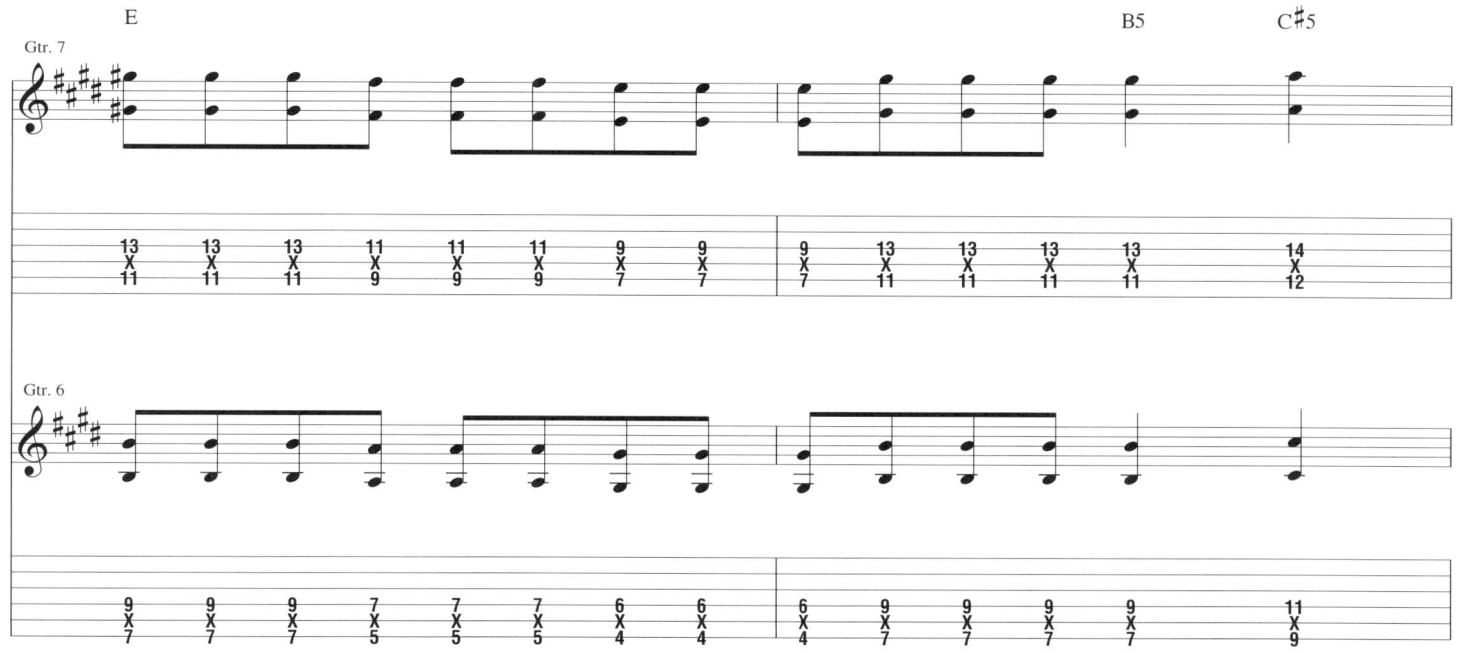

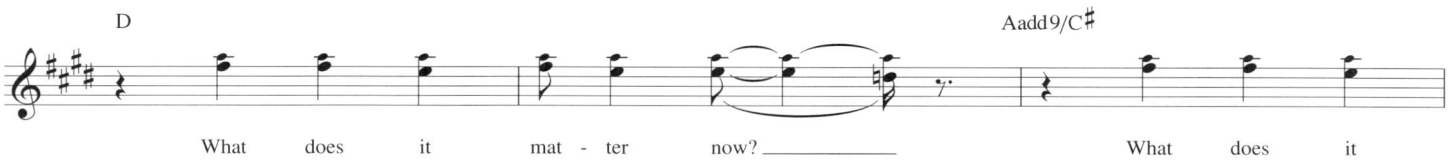

What does it matter now? _____ What does it

mat- ter now? _____ It's just a mat- ter of _____ time. ____

Outro

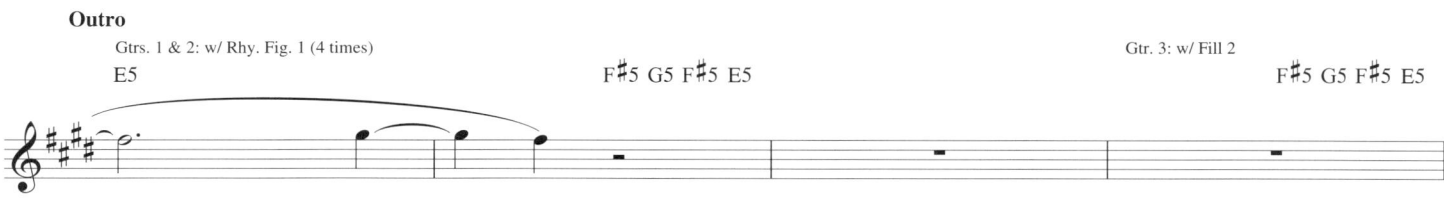

Screamed: Time. _____

Miss the Misery

Words and Music by David Grohl, Taylor Hawkins, Christopher Shiflett, Nate Mendel and Pat Smear

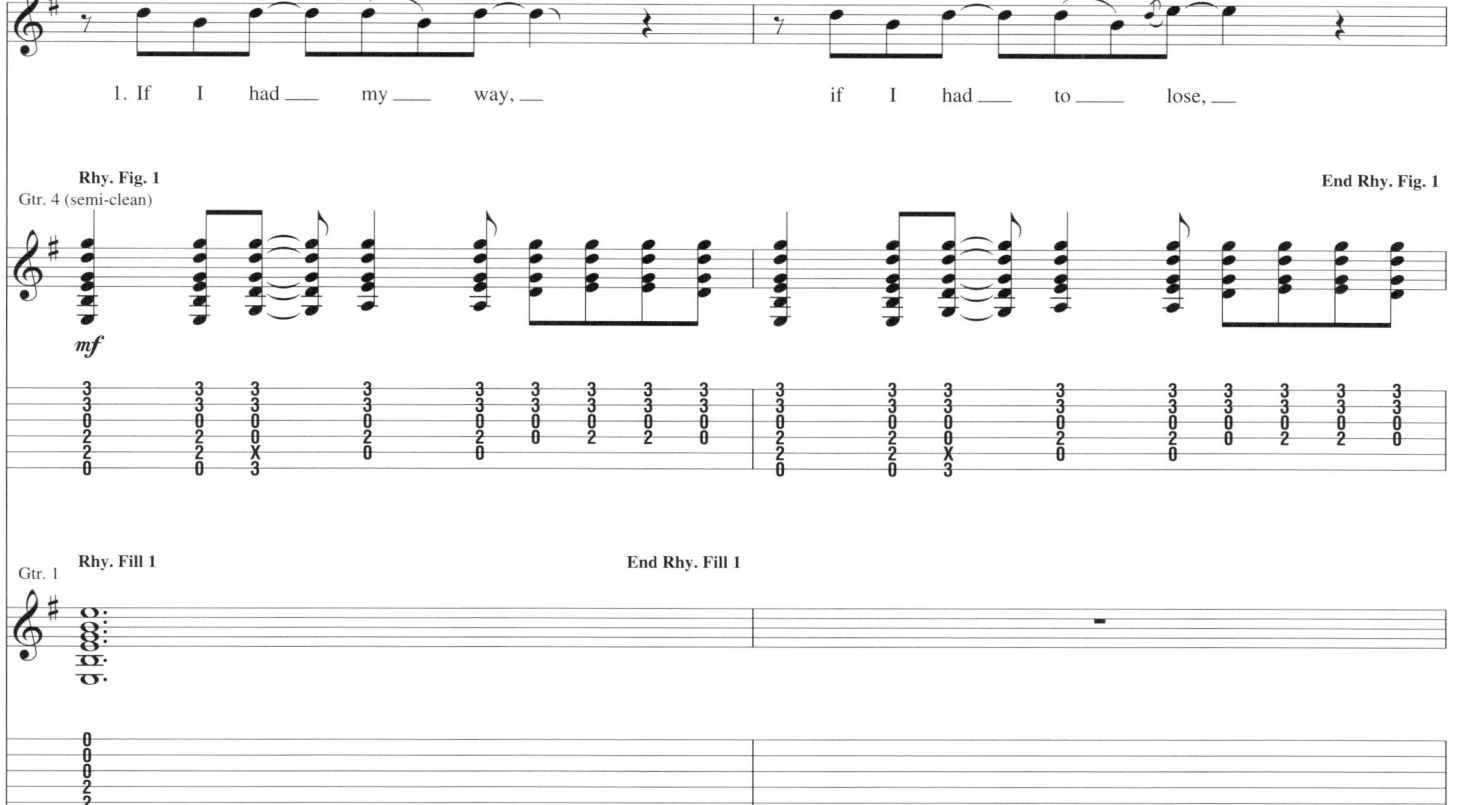
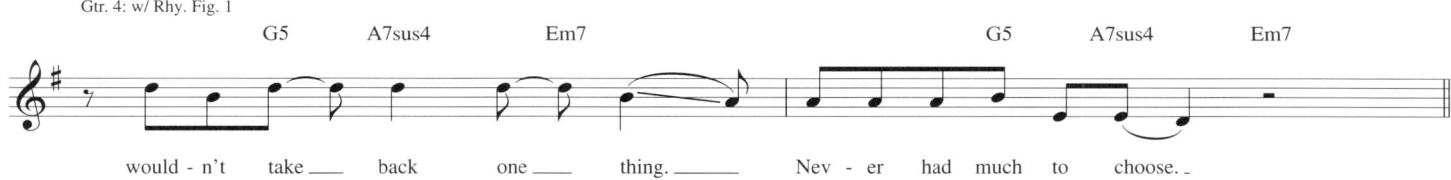
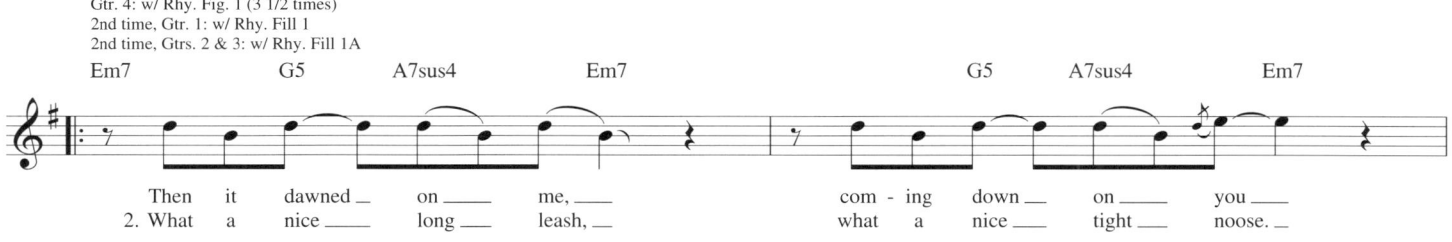

93

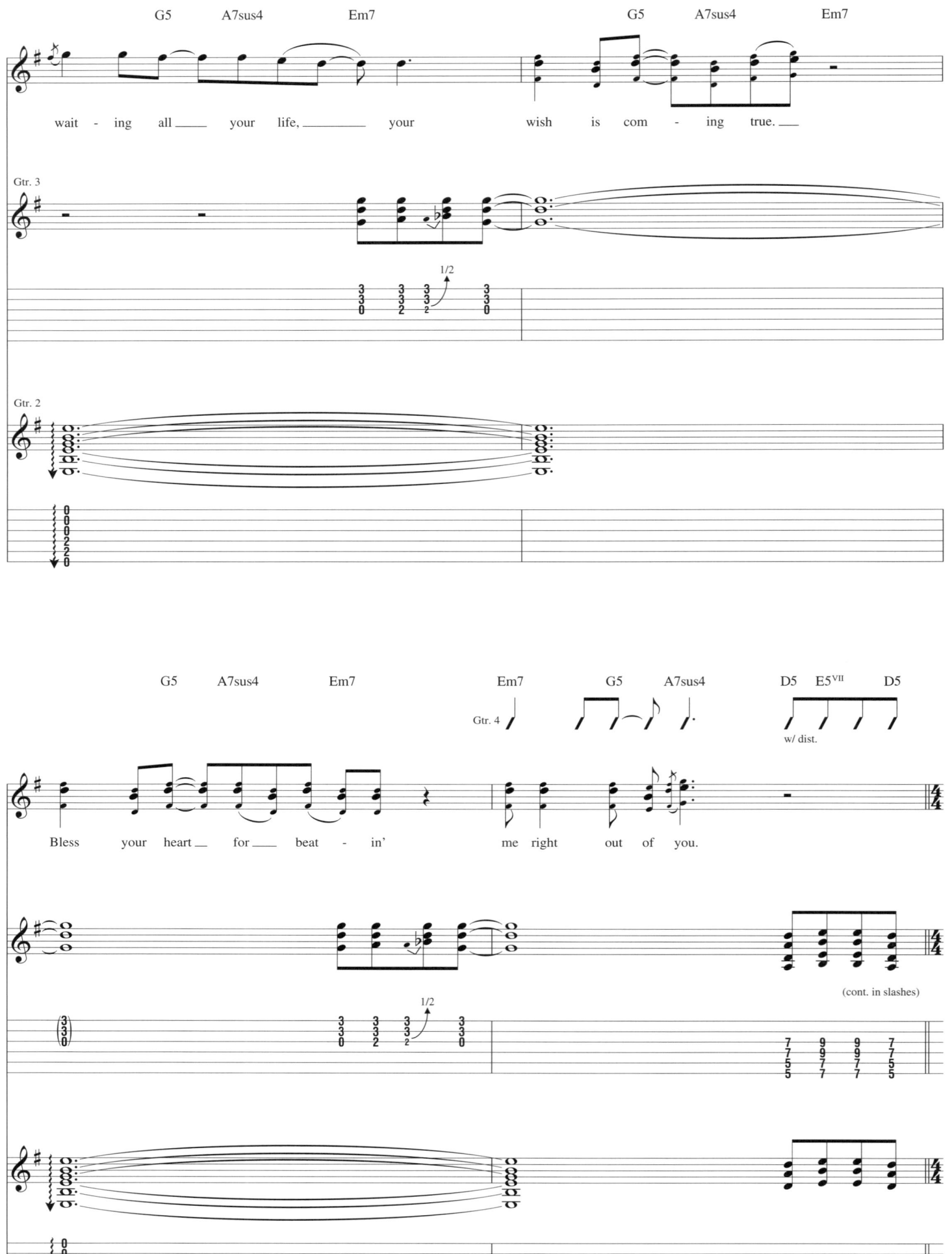

Pre-Chorus
C5
D5
E5 VII
B5
Rhy. Fig. 2
End Rhy. Fig. 2
Gtrs. 3 & 4
Miss the mis - er - y, need a rea - son for a change.
Gtr. 2
Gtrs. 3 & 4: w/ Rhy. Fig. 2
C5
D5
E5
B5
Need a rea - son to { ex - plain, / re - frain, } so turn it on a - gain.
Chorus
Csus2
D
Em7
B5
Don't change your mind. You're wast - in' light.
Rhy. Fig. 3
End Rhy. Fig. 3
Gtrs. 2, 3 & 4

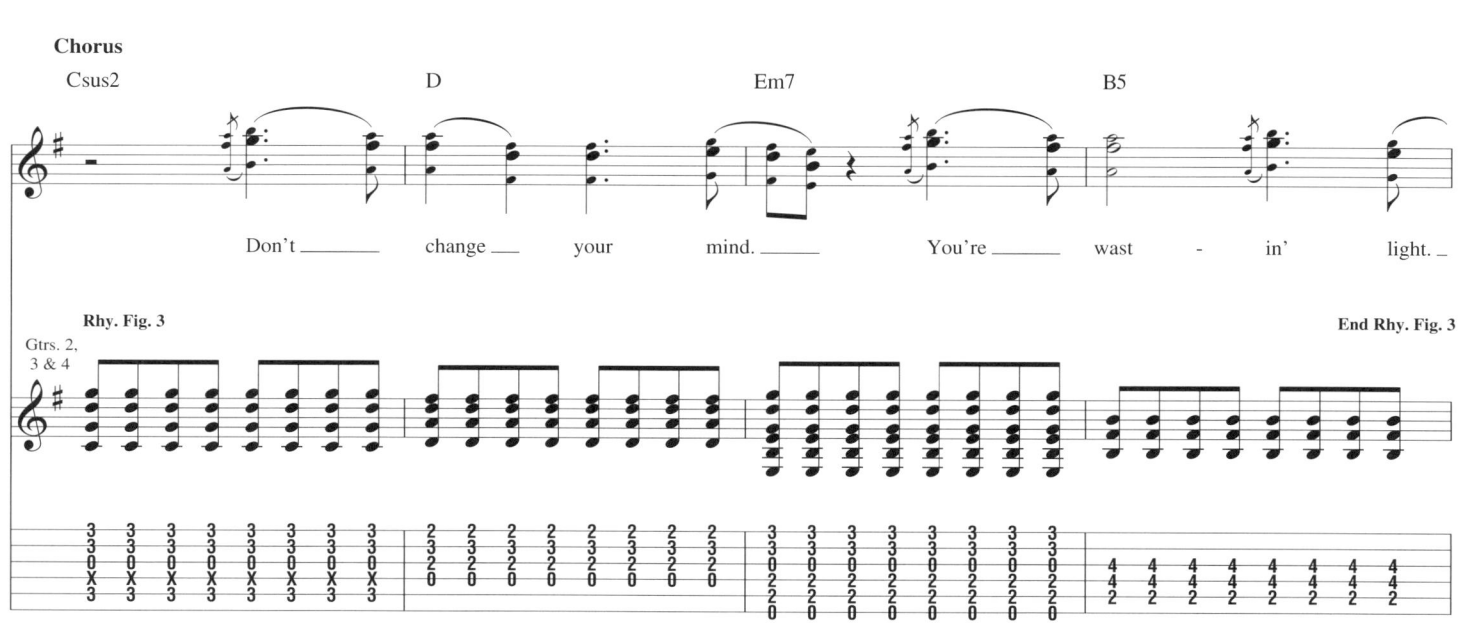

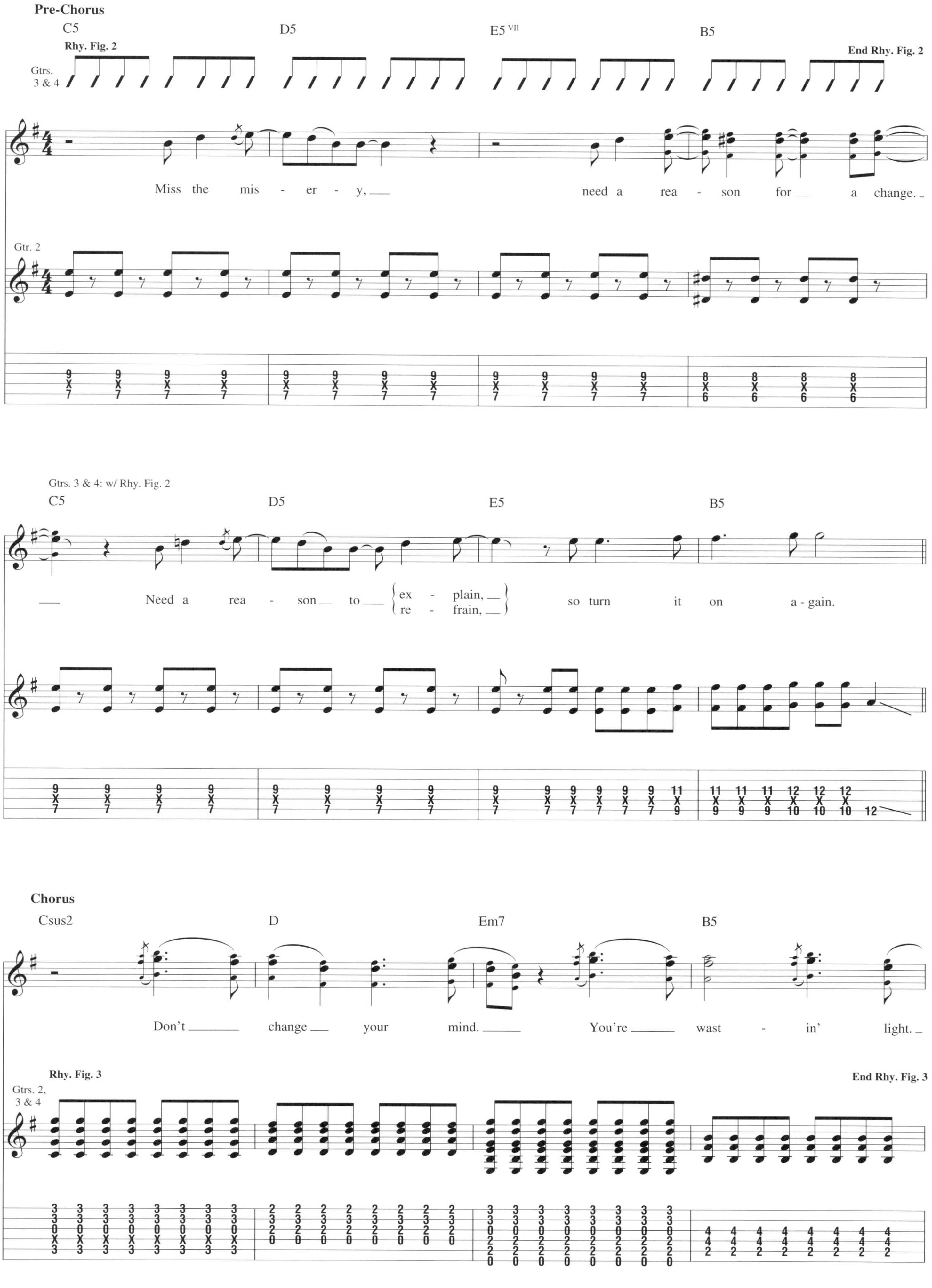

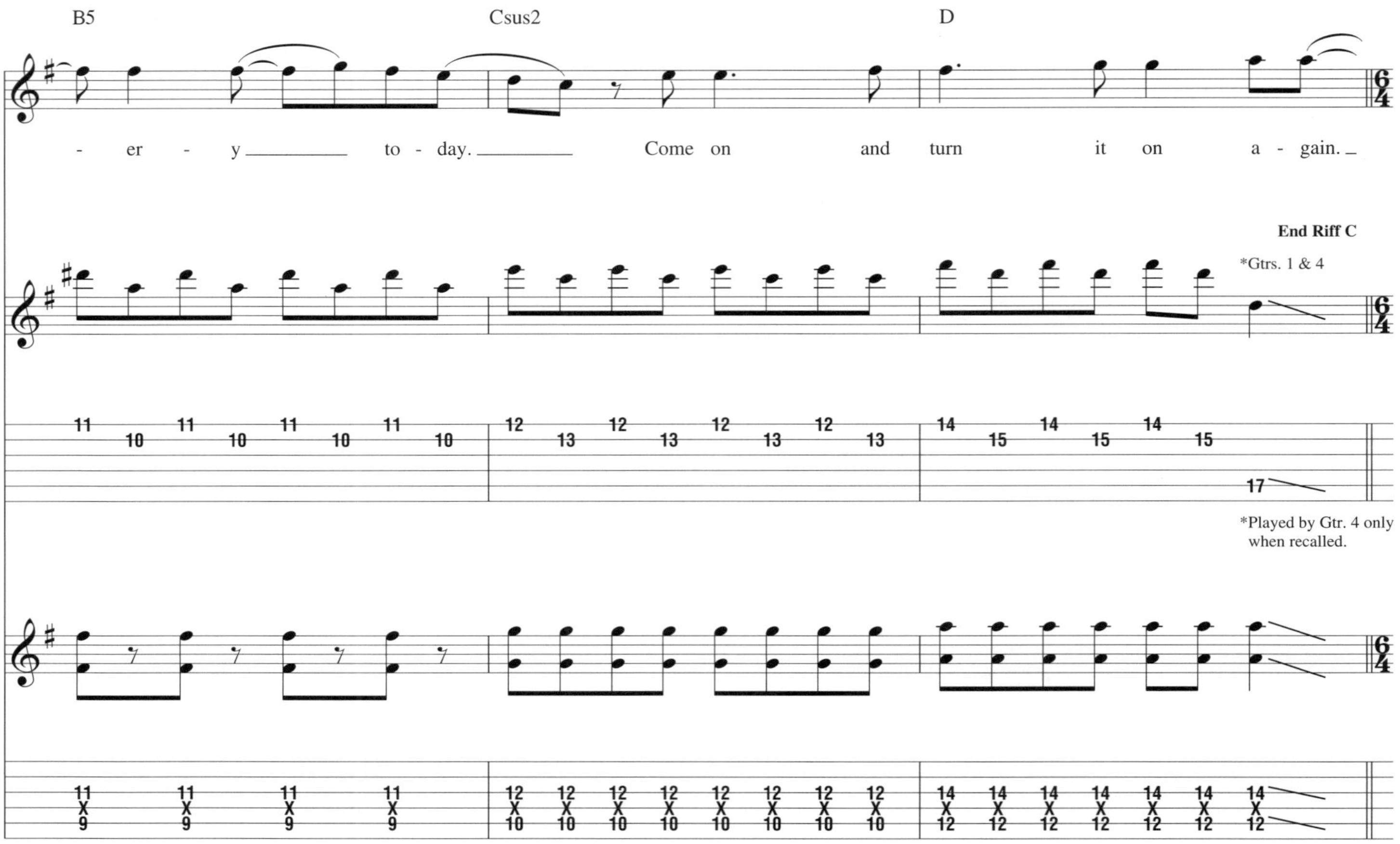
B5
Csus2
D
- er - y to - day. Come on and turn it on a - gain.
End Riff C
*Gtrs. 1 & 4
*Played by Gtr. 4 only when recalled.

Interlude

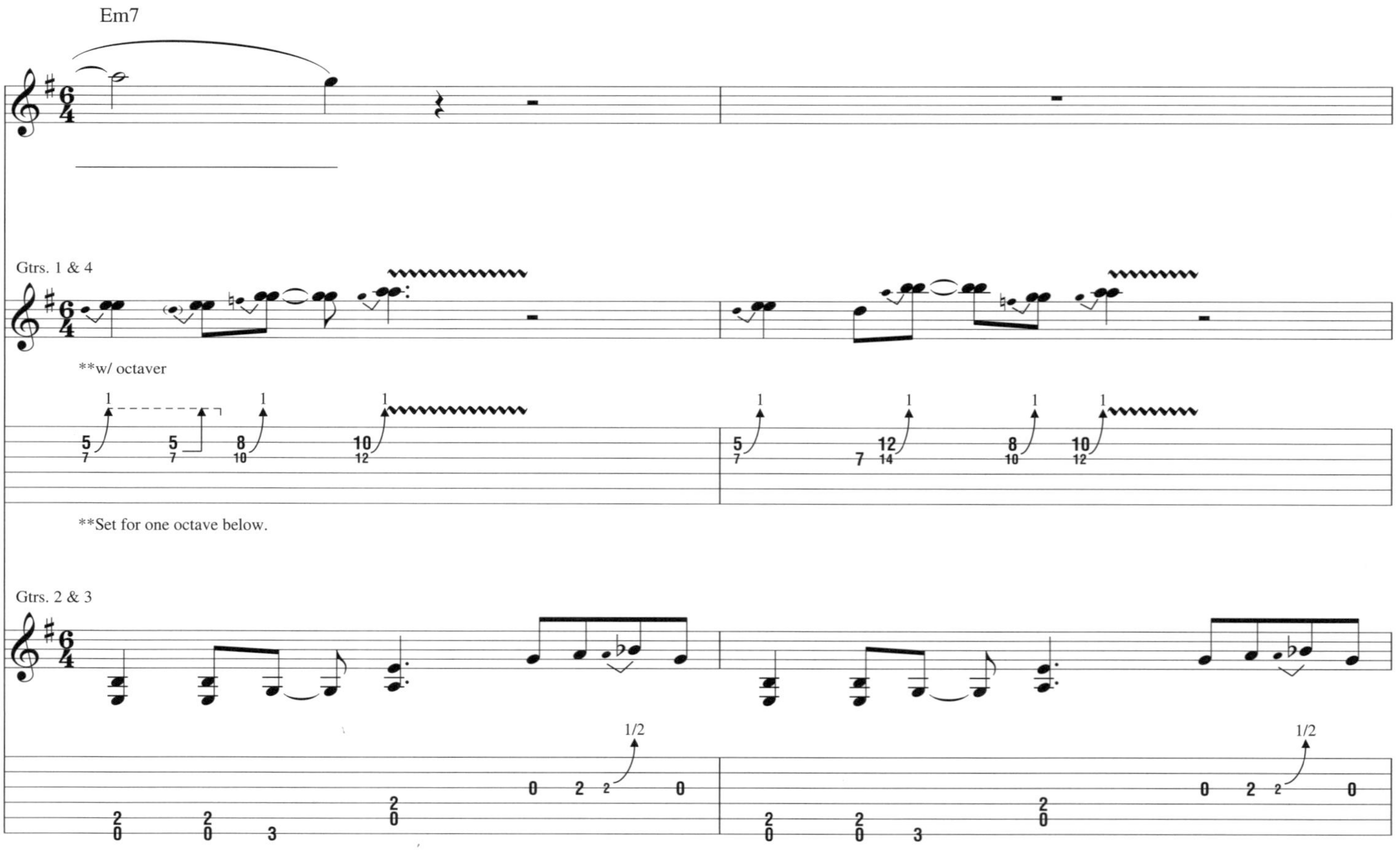
Em7
Gtrs. 1 & 4
**w/ octaver
**Set for one octave below.
Gtrs. 2 & 3

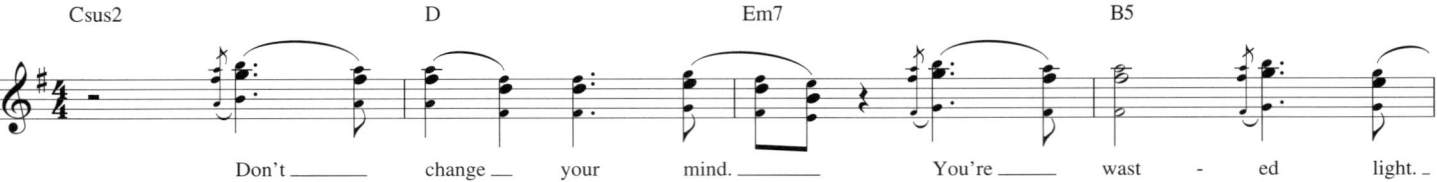
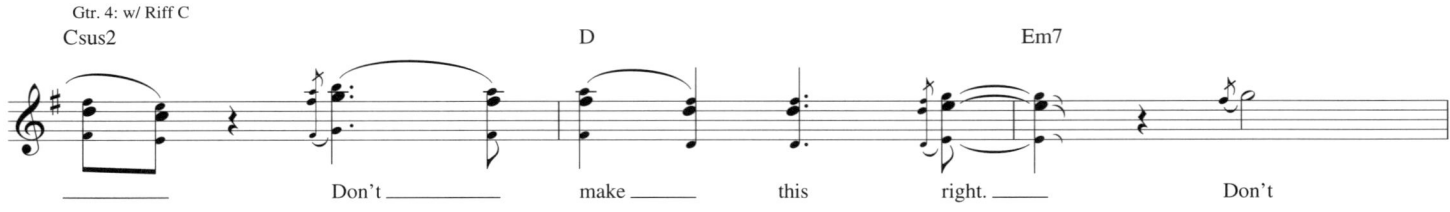
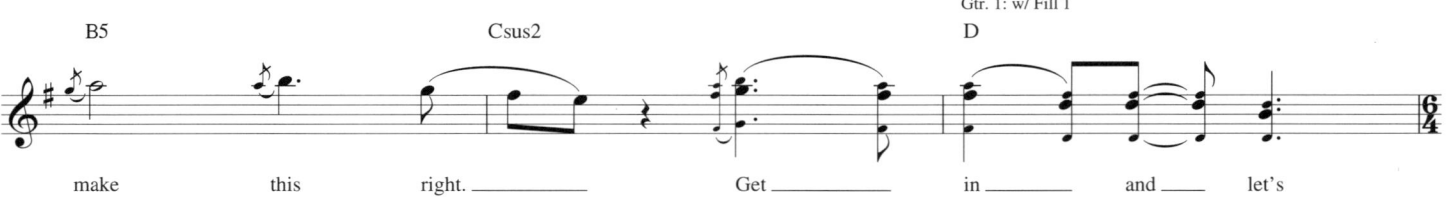
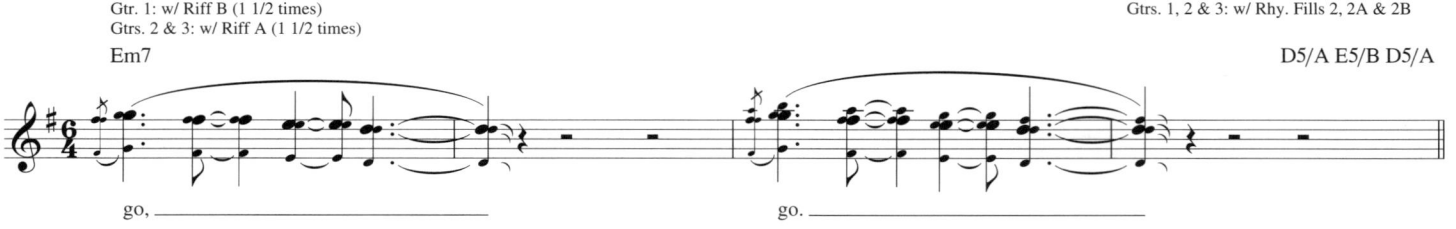
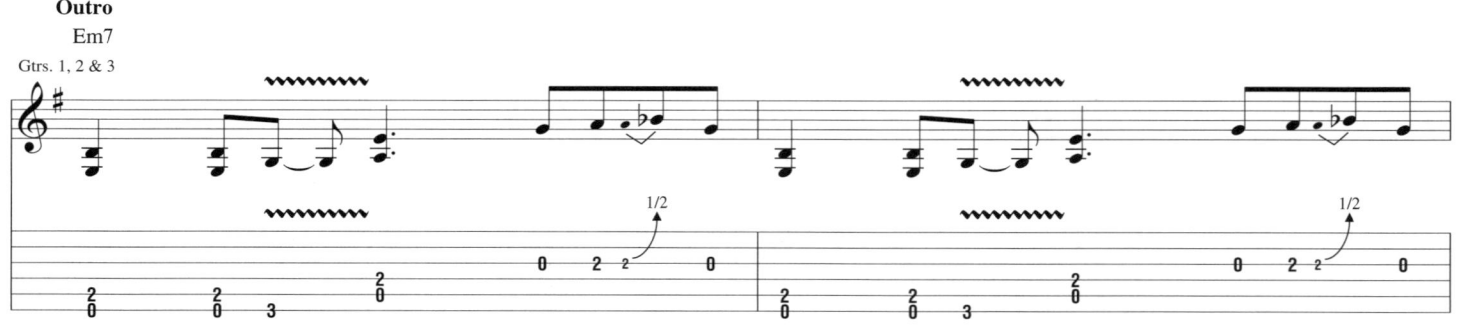
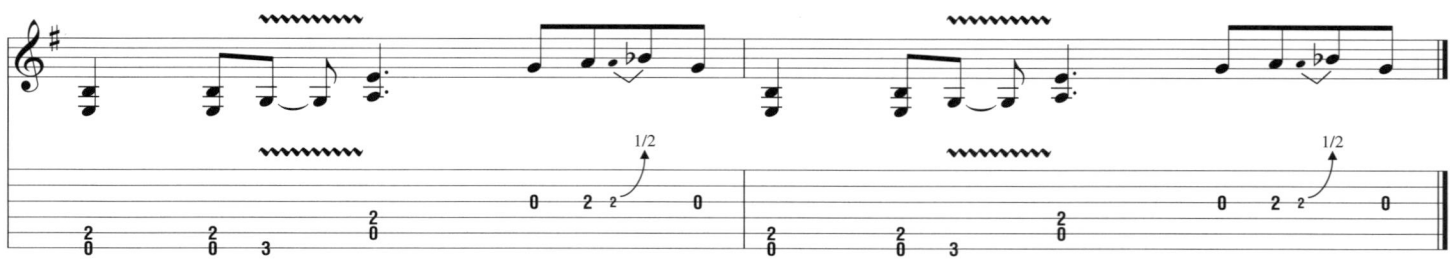

I Should Have Known

Words and Music by David Grohl, Taylor Hawkins, Christopher Shiflett, Nate Mendel and Pat Smear

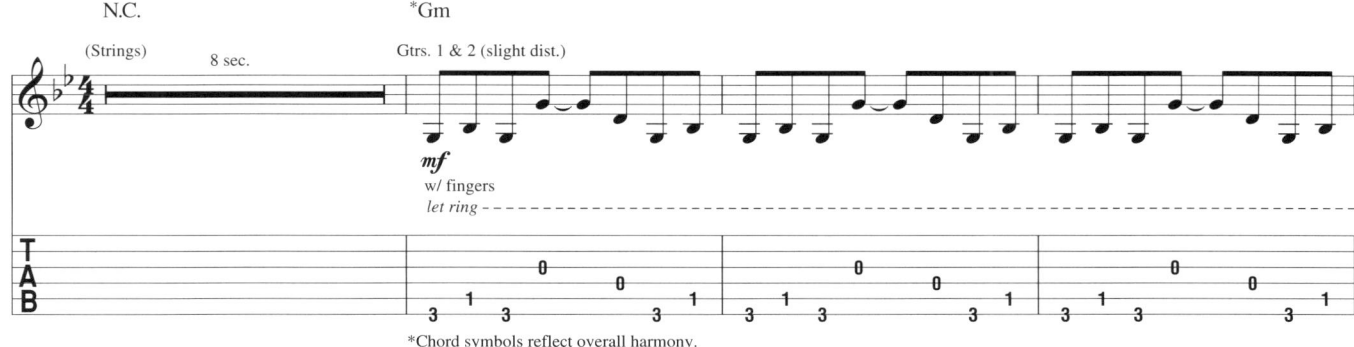

Copyright © 2011 SONGS OF UNIVERSAL, INC., MJ TWELVE MUSIC, LIVING UNDER A ROCK MUSIC,
I LOVE THE PUNK ROCK MUSIC, FLYING EARFORM MUSIC and RUTHENSMEAR MUSIC
All Rights for MJ TWELVE MUSIC and I LOVE THE PUNK ROCK MUSIC Controlled and Administered by SONGS OF UNIVERSAL, INC.
All Rights for LIVING UNDER A ROCK MUSIC Controlled and Administered by UNIVERSAL MUSIC CORP.
All Rights for FLYING EARFORM MUSIC and RUTHENSMEAR MUSIC Administered by BUG MUSIC
All Rights Reserved   Used by Permission

Gtr. 1: w/ Rhy. Fig. 2 (2 times)
Gtr. 2: w/ Riff C
Gm Fadd9/A B♭ Gm7/F C
Lay your hands in mine.
Gm Fadd9/A B♭ Gm7/F C
Feel me one last time. Though I can-
Gtr. 2
let ring
Chorus
E♭ Gm E♭
not for - give you yet. No, I can - not for - give you yet.
Rhy. Fig. 3
Gtr. 1
let ring
Riff D
Gtr. 2
let ring

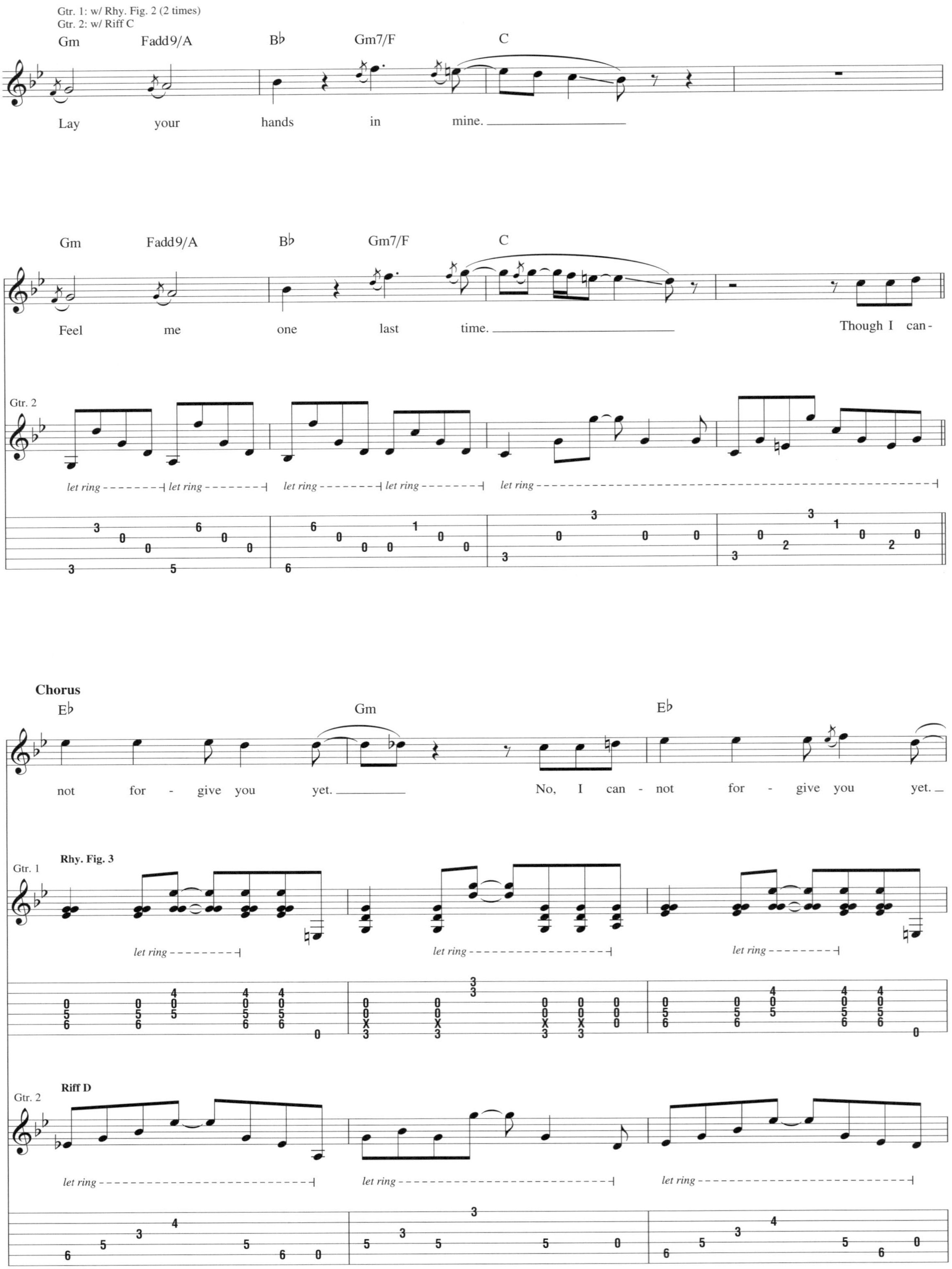

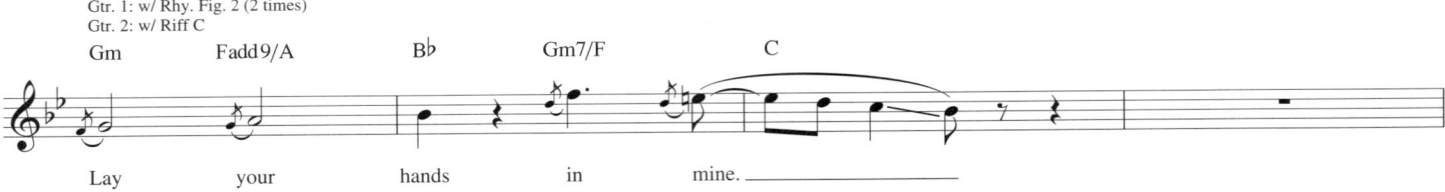

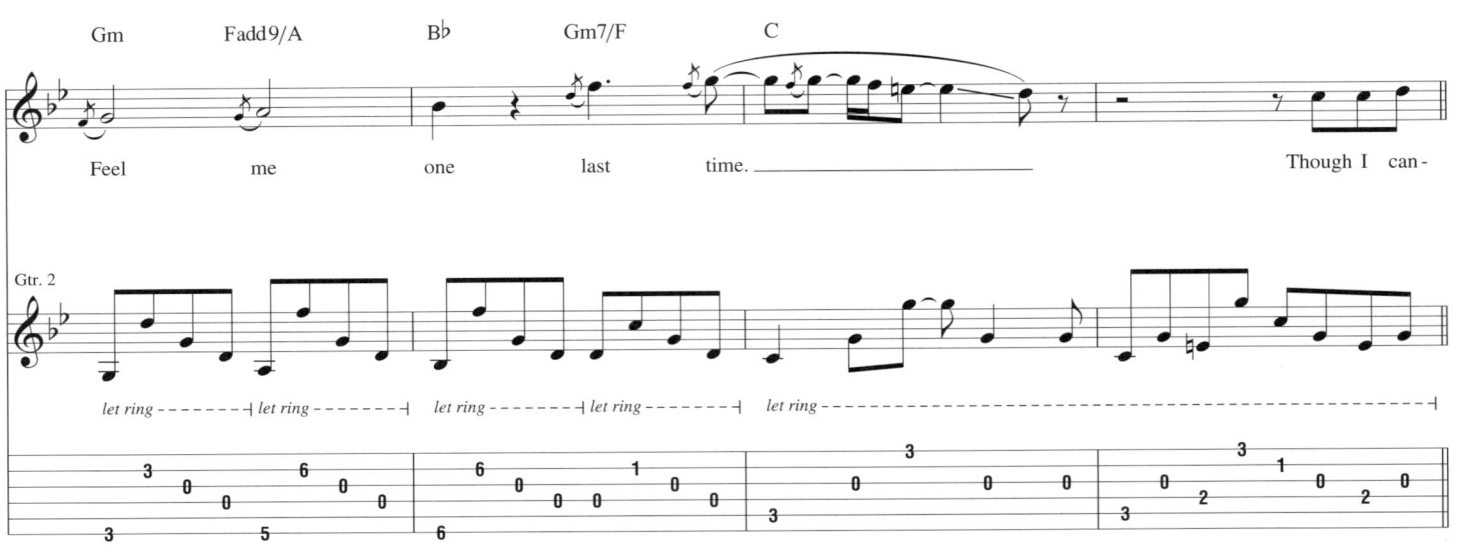

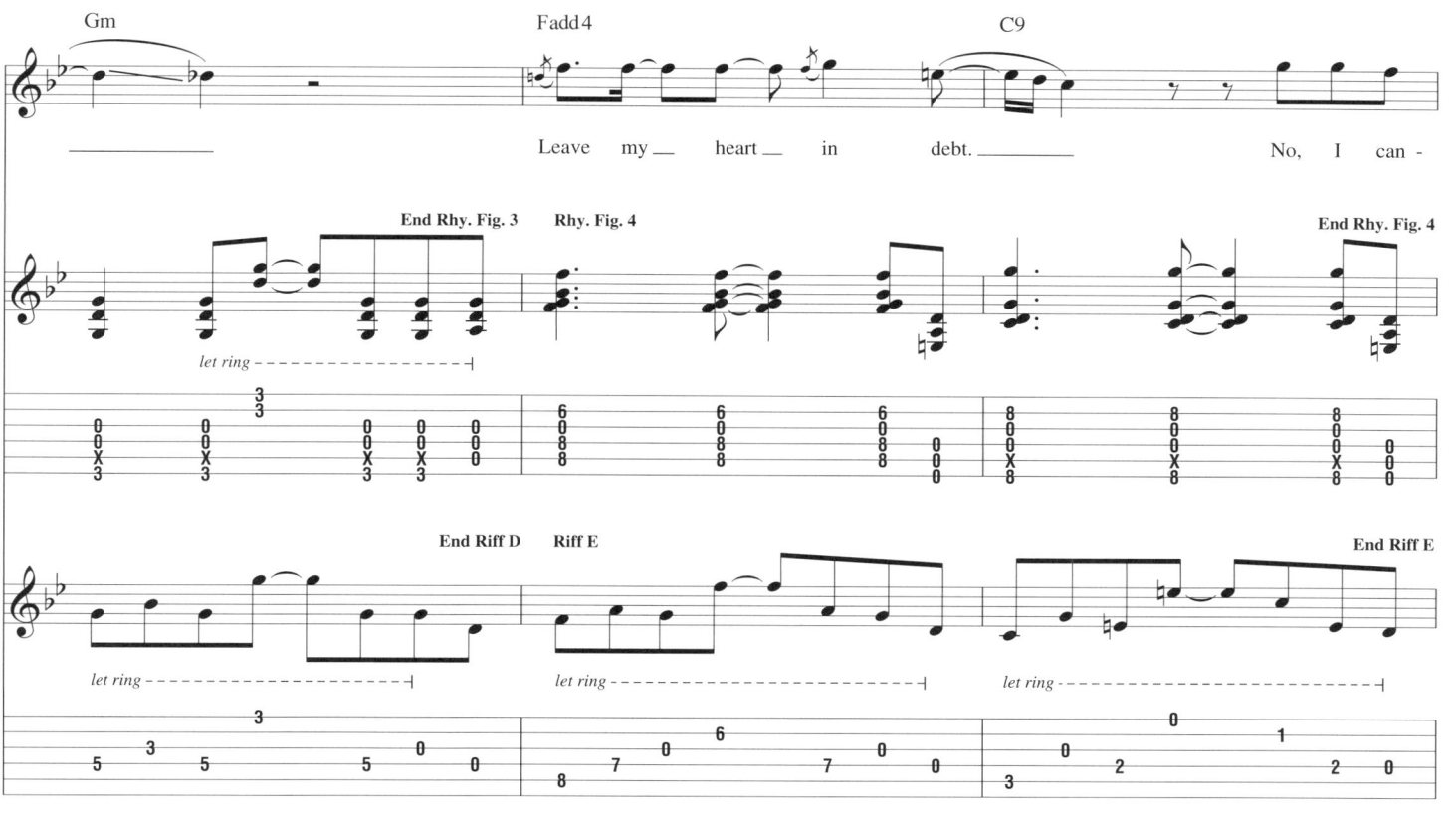
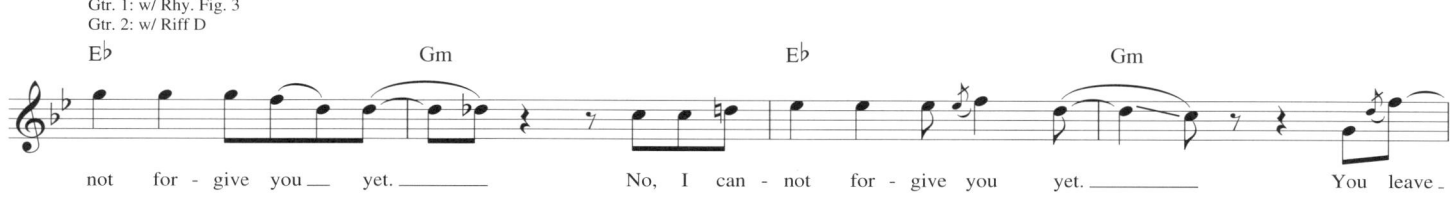
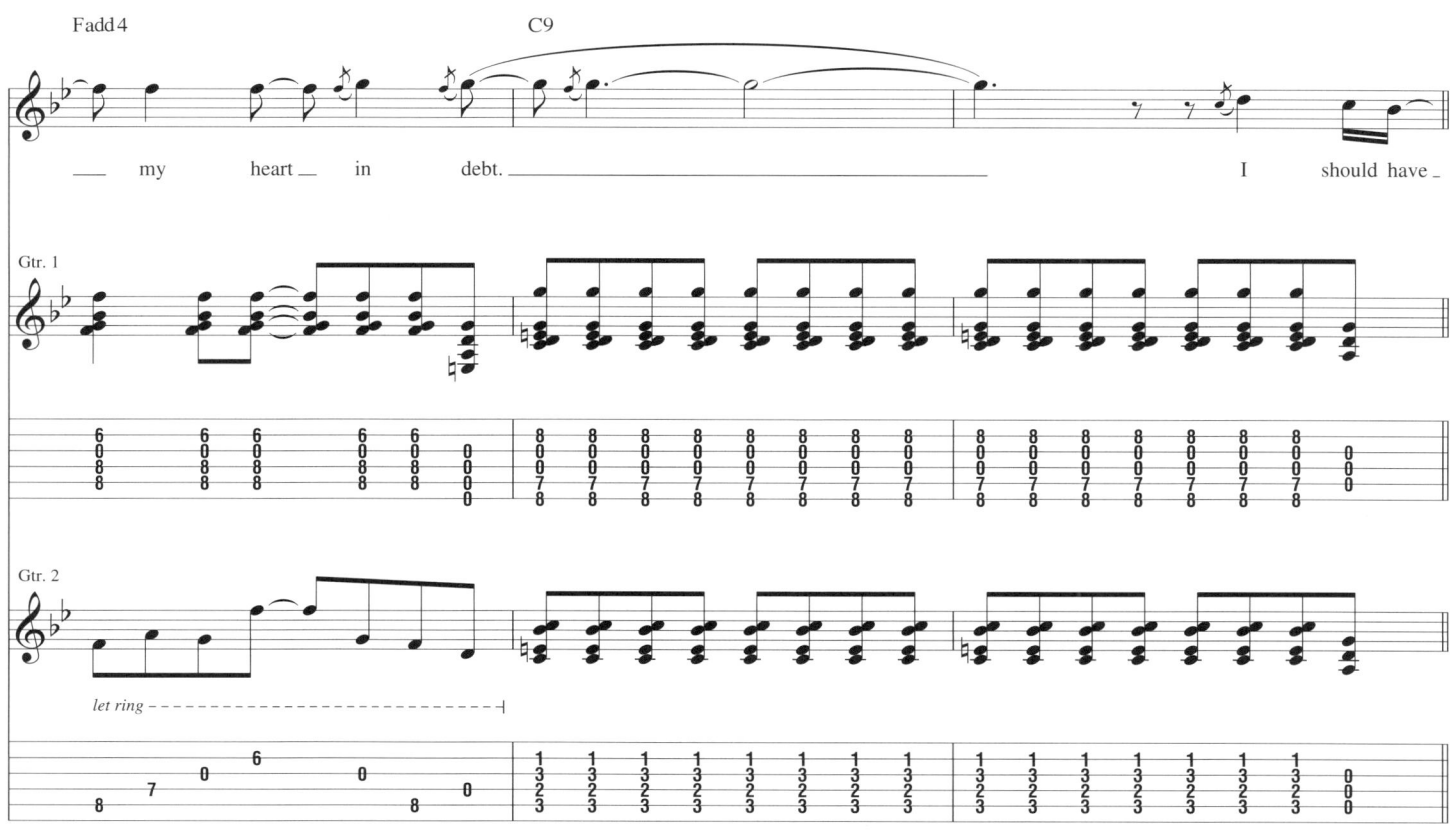

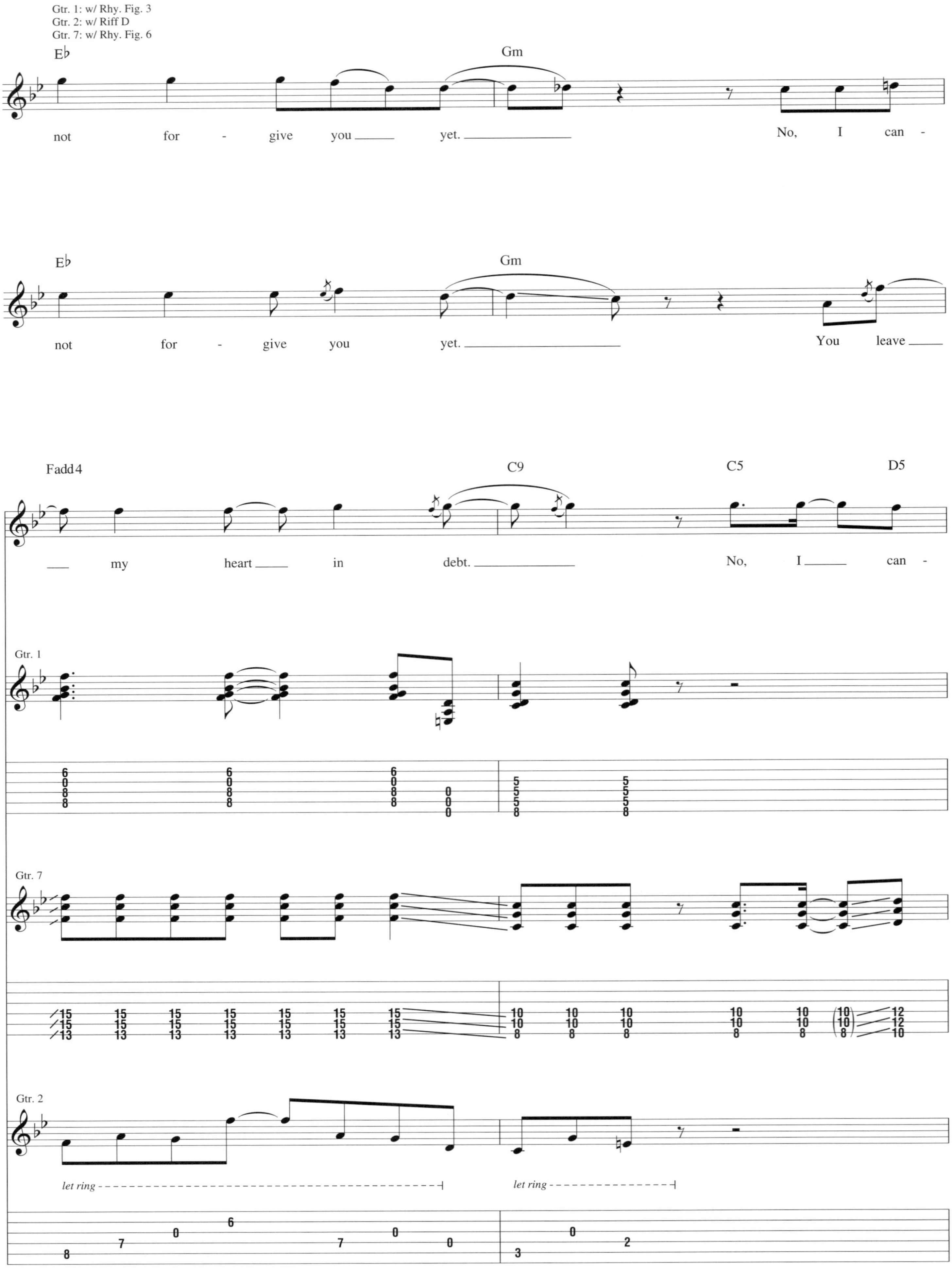
Gtr. 1: w/ Rhy. Fig. 3
Gtr. 2: w/ Riff D
Gtr. 7: w/ Rhy. Fig. 6
E♭
Gm
not for - give you yet. No, I can -
E♭
Gm
not for - give you yet. You leave
Fadd4
C9
C5
D5
my heart in debt. No, I can -
Gtr. 1
Gtr. 7
Gtr. 2
let ring
let ring

Walk

Words and Music by David Grohl, Taylor Hawkins, Christopher Shiflett, Nate Mendel and Pat Smear

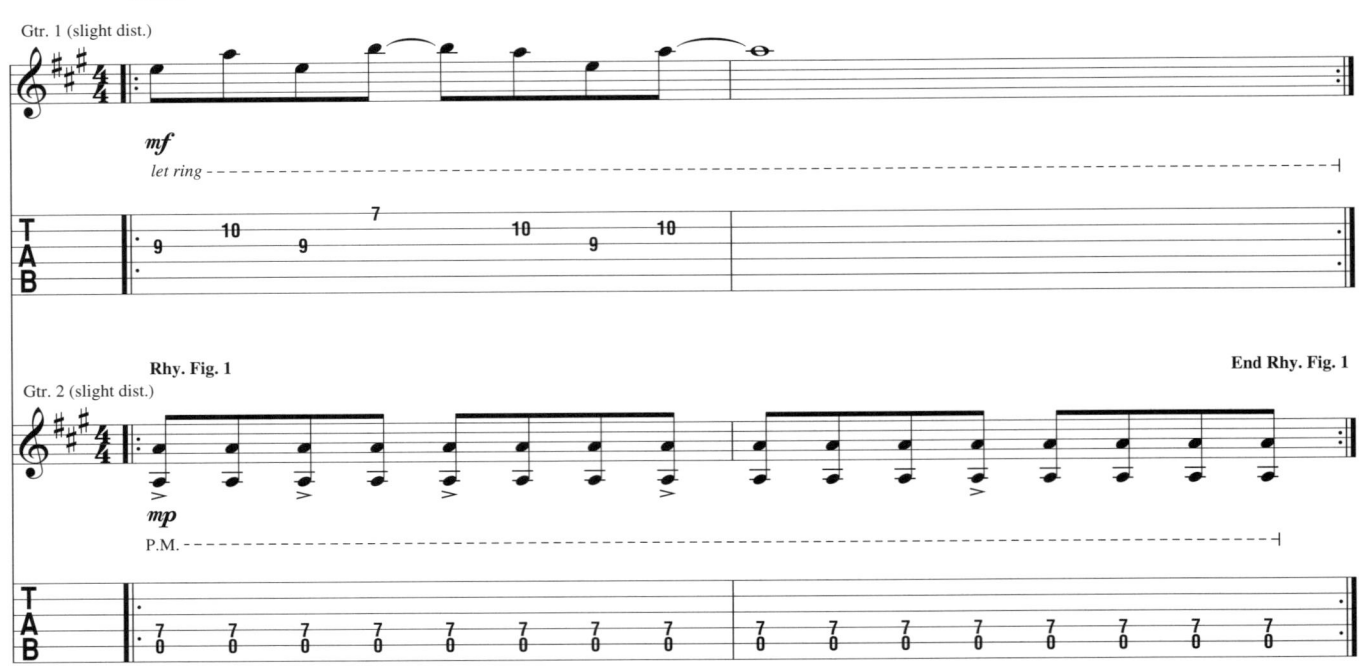

*Chord symbols reflect overall harmony.

Verse

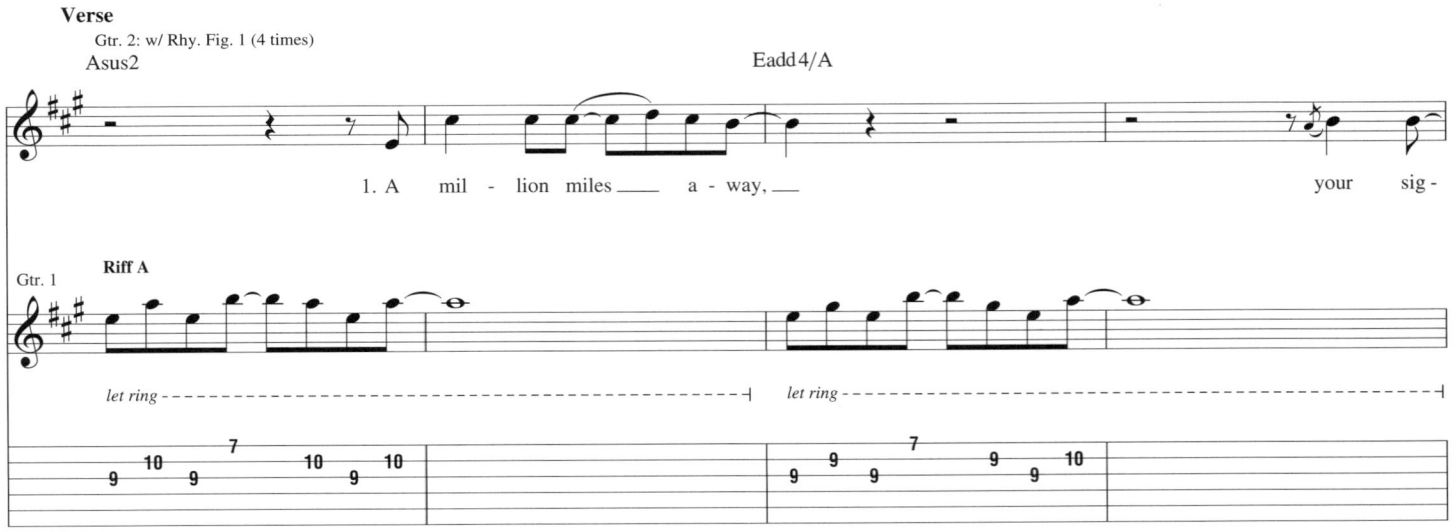

1. A million miles away, your sig-

Copyright © 2011 SONGS OF UNIVERSAL, INC., MJ TWELVE MUSIC, LIVING UNDER A ROCK MUSIC,
I LOVE THE PUNK ROCK MUSIC, FLYING EARFORM MUSIC and RUTHENSMEAR MUSIC
All Rights for MJ TWELVE MUSIC and I LOVE THE PUNK ROCK MUSIC Controlled and Administered by SONGS OF UNIVERSAL, INC.
All Rights for LIVING UNDER A ROCK MUSIC Controlled and Administered by UNIVERSAL MUSIC CORP.
All Rights for FLYING EARFORM MUSIC and RUTHENSMEAR MUSIC Administered by BUG MUSIC
All Rights Reserved   Used by Permission

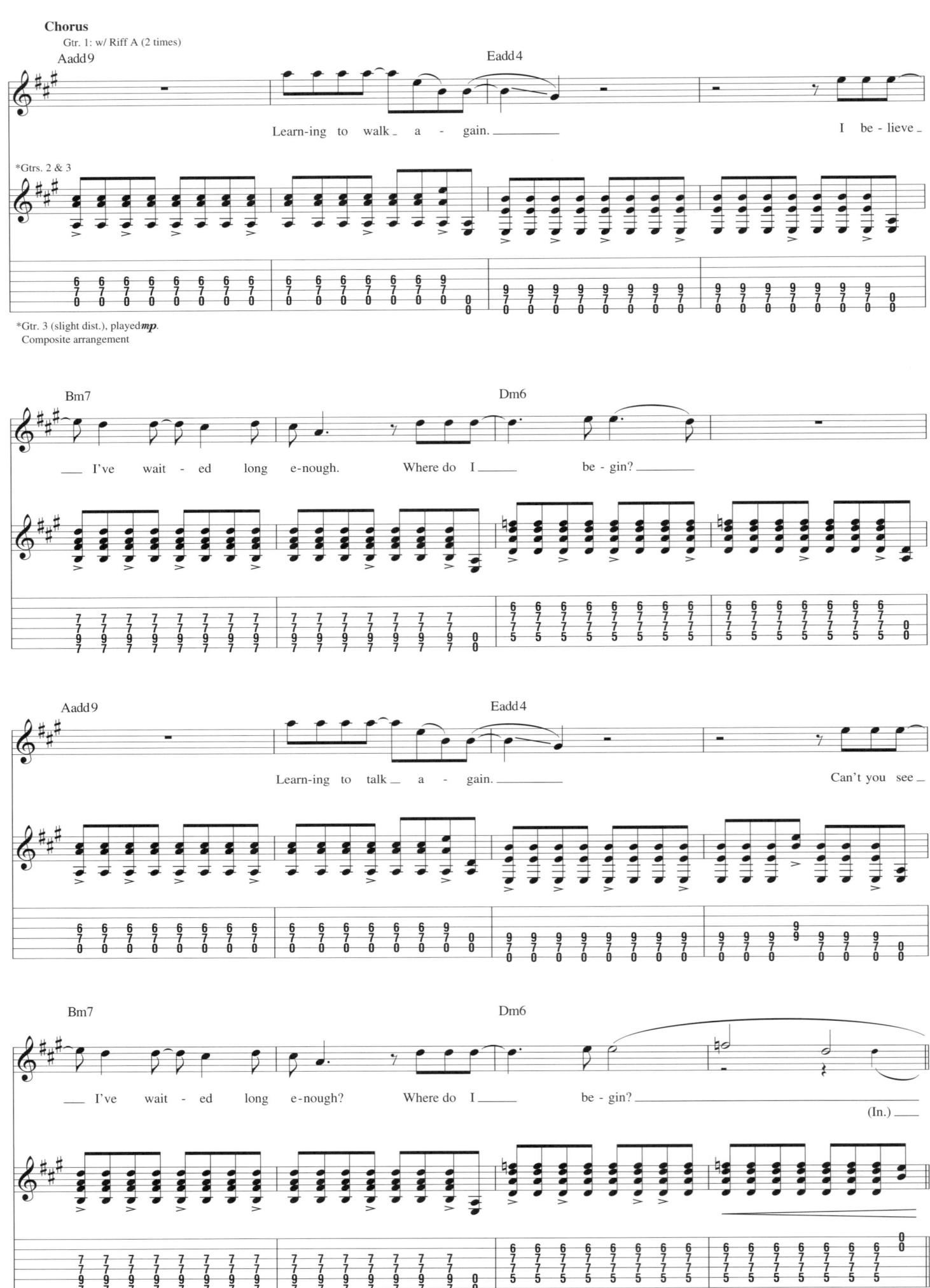

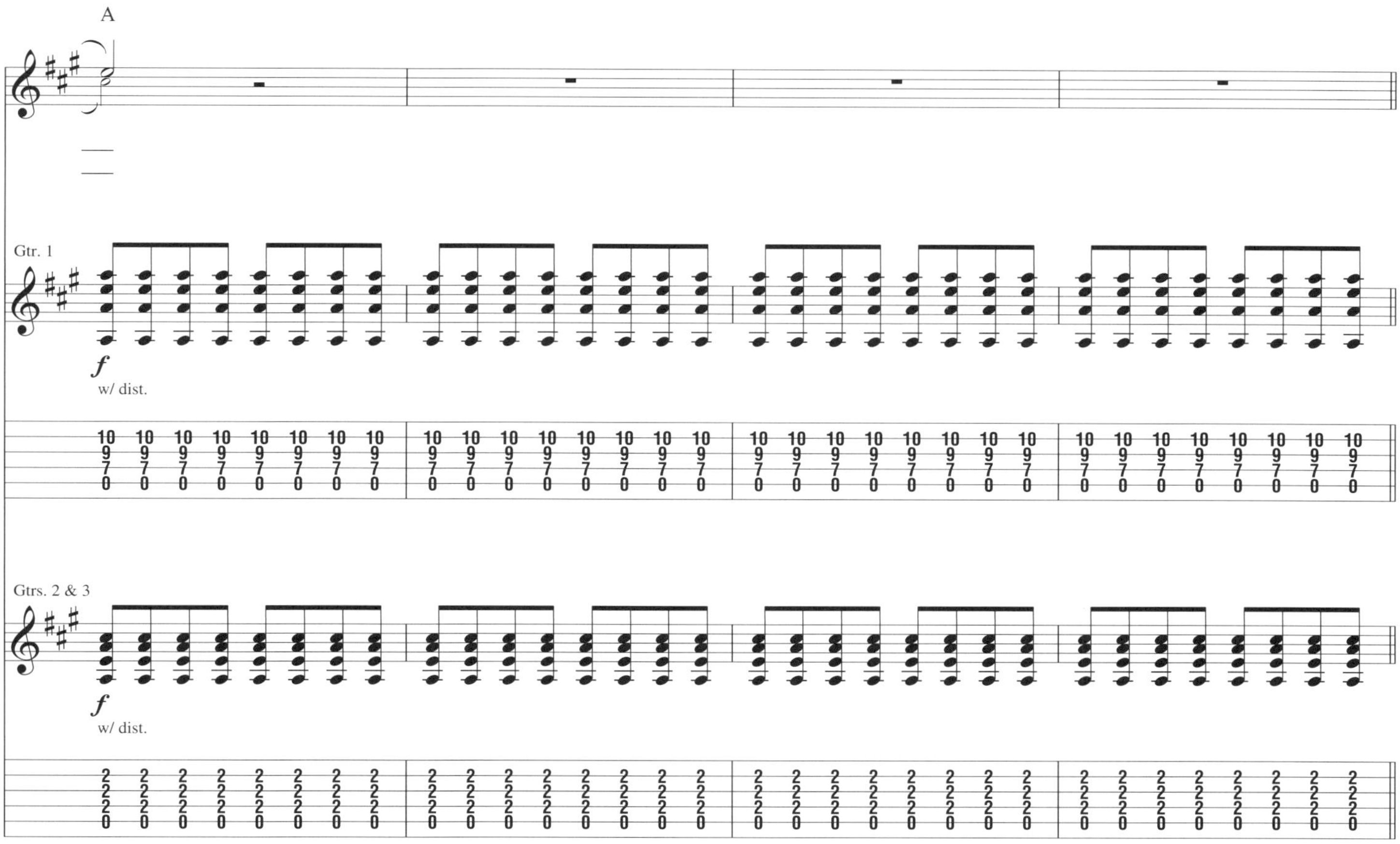

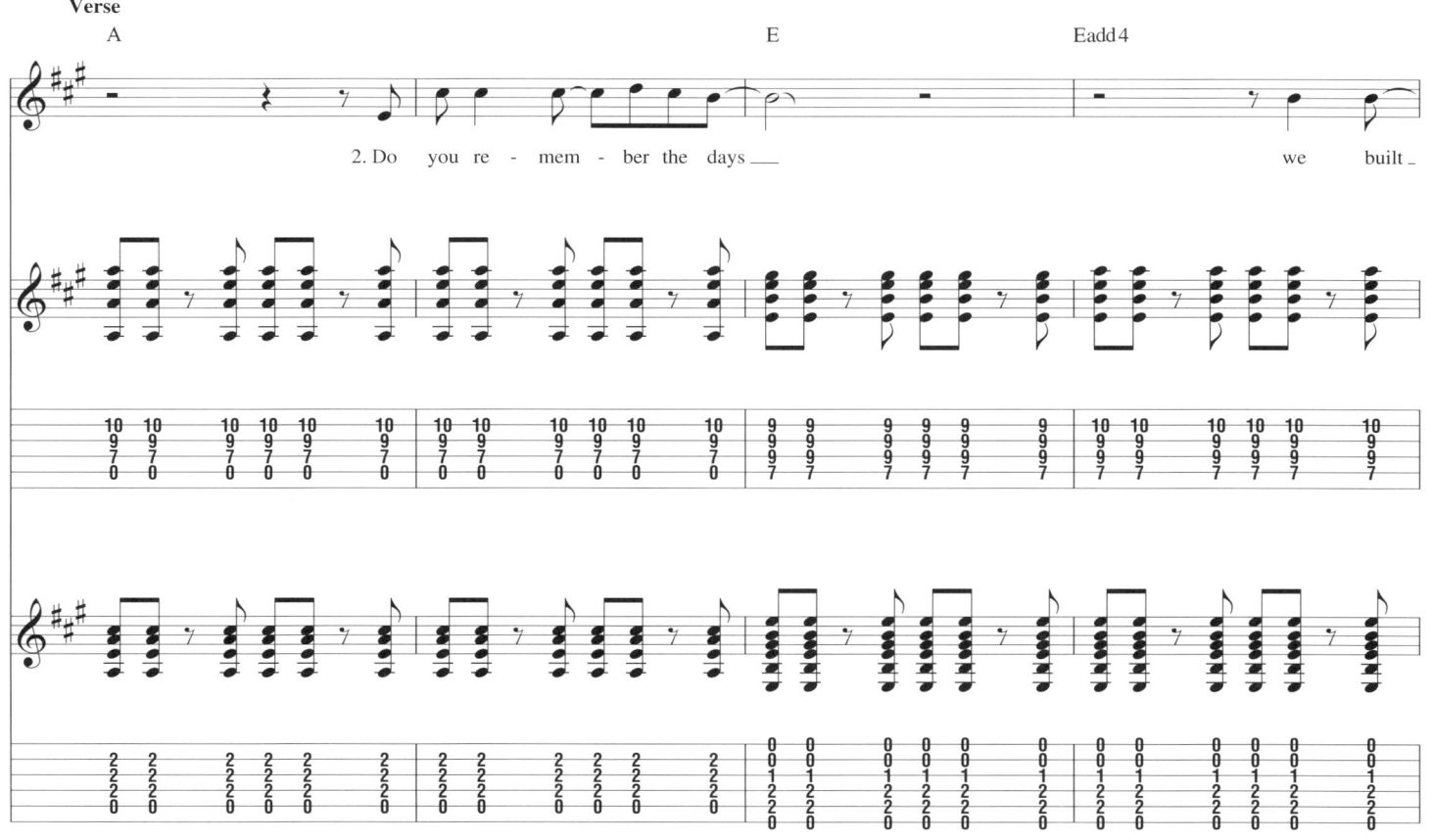

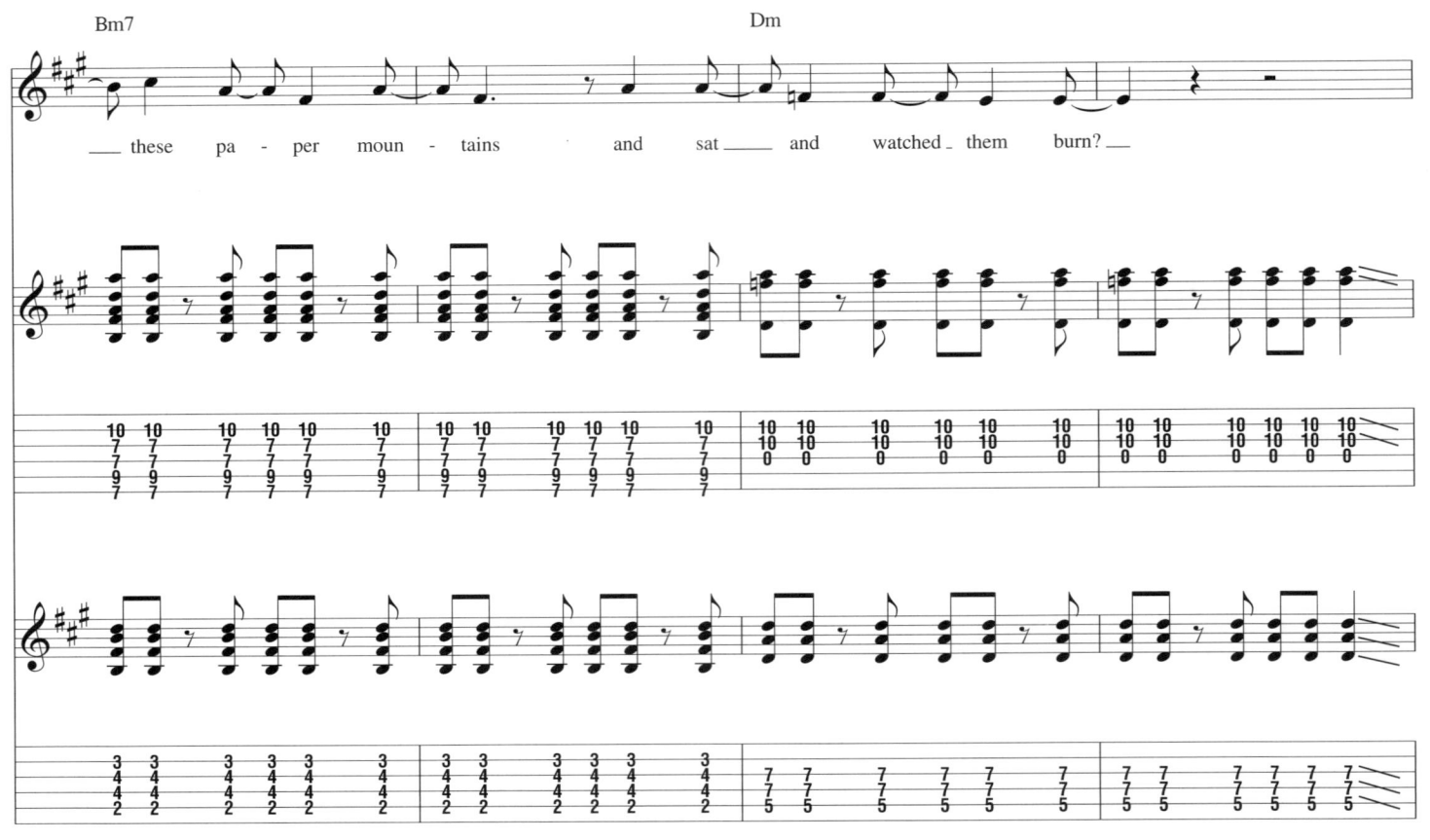
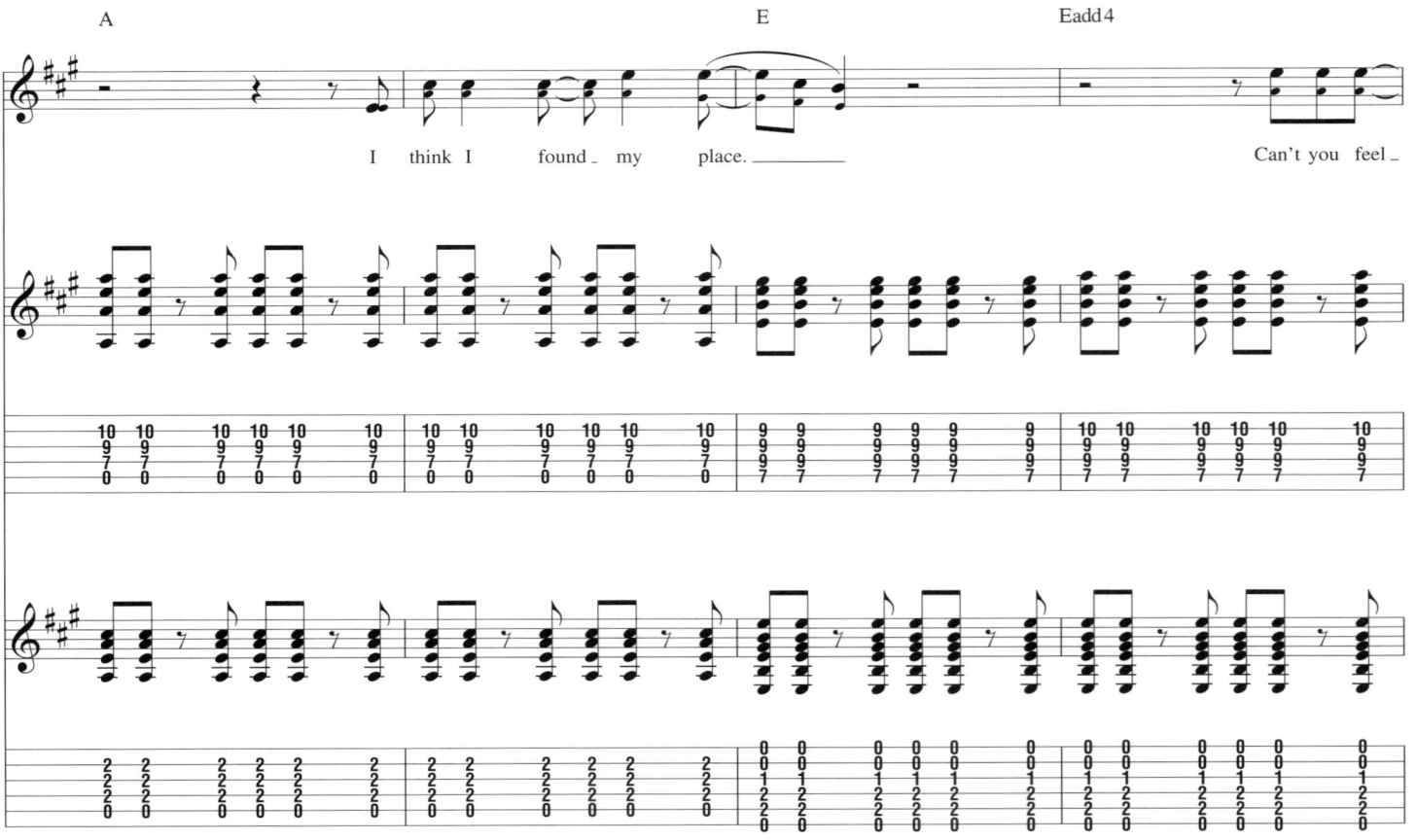

Bm7
Dm
Dm/E
Dm/F
Dm/G
it grow - ing strong - er, lit - tle con - quer - ors?
Chorus
A
E
Eadd4
Learn-ing to walk a - gain.
I be - lieve
Rhy. Fig. 2
Rhy. Fig. 2A
let ring

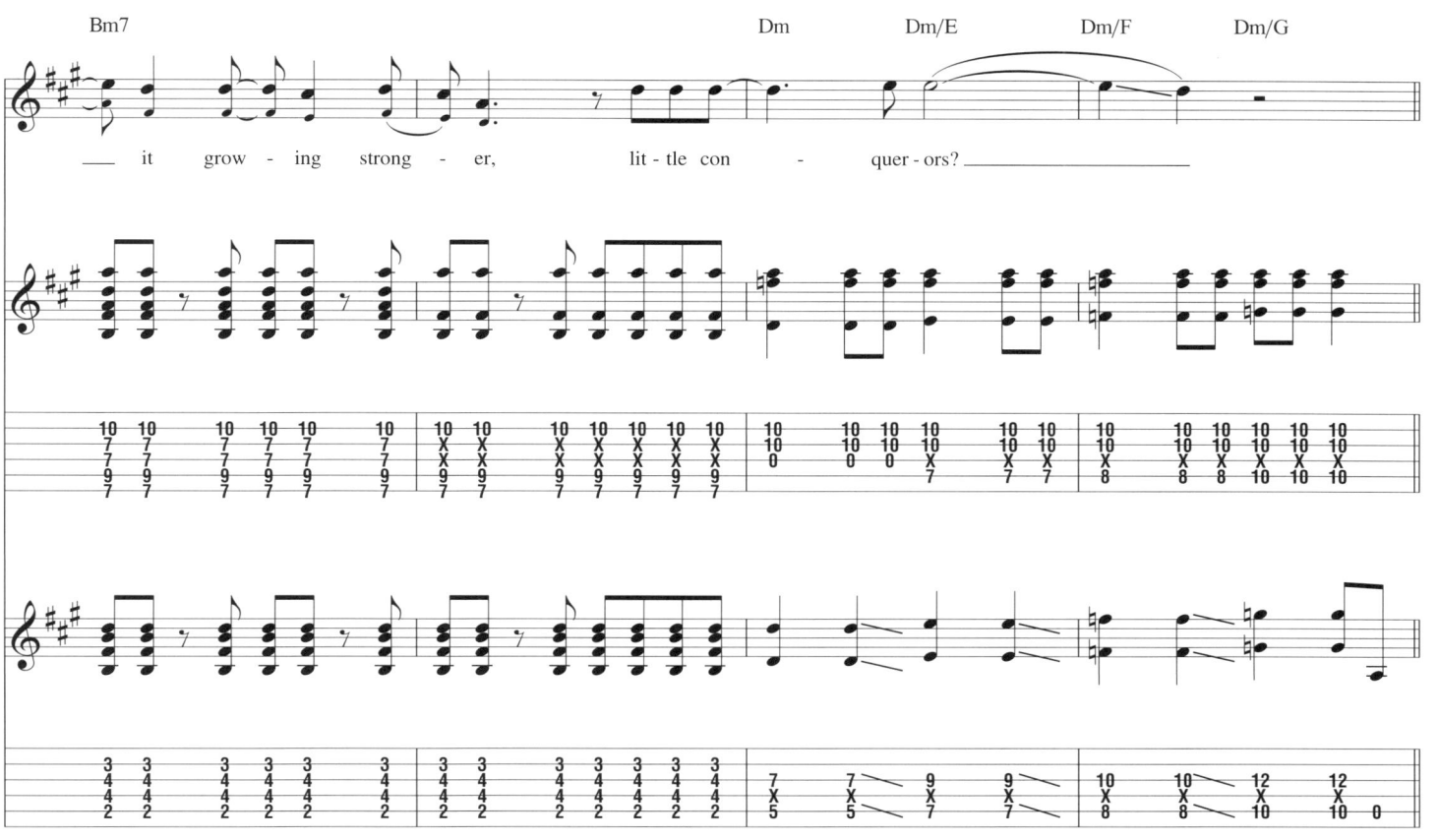

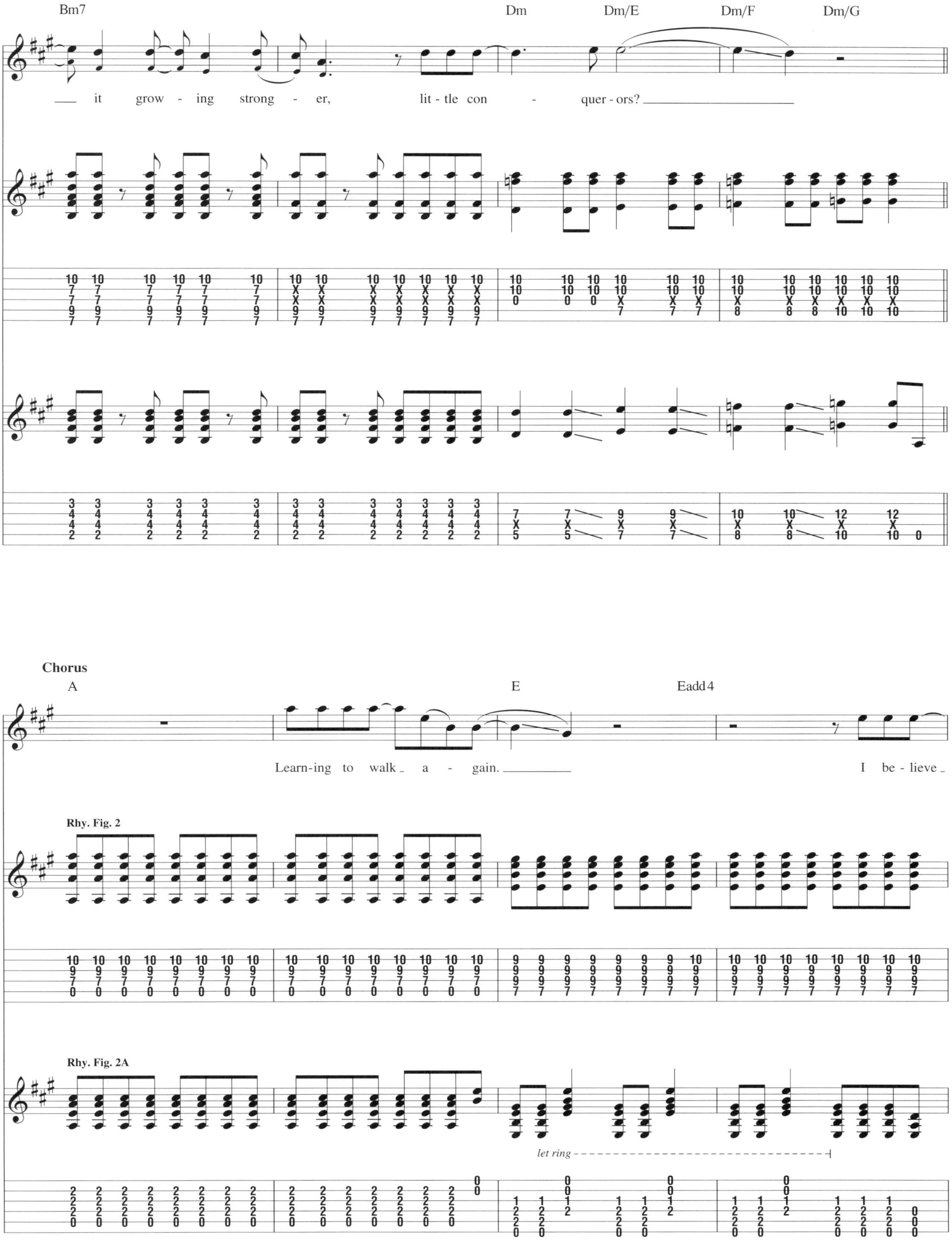

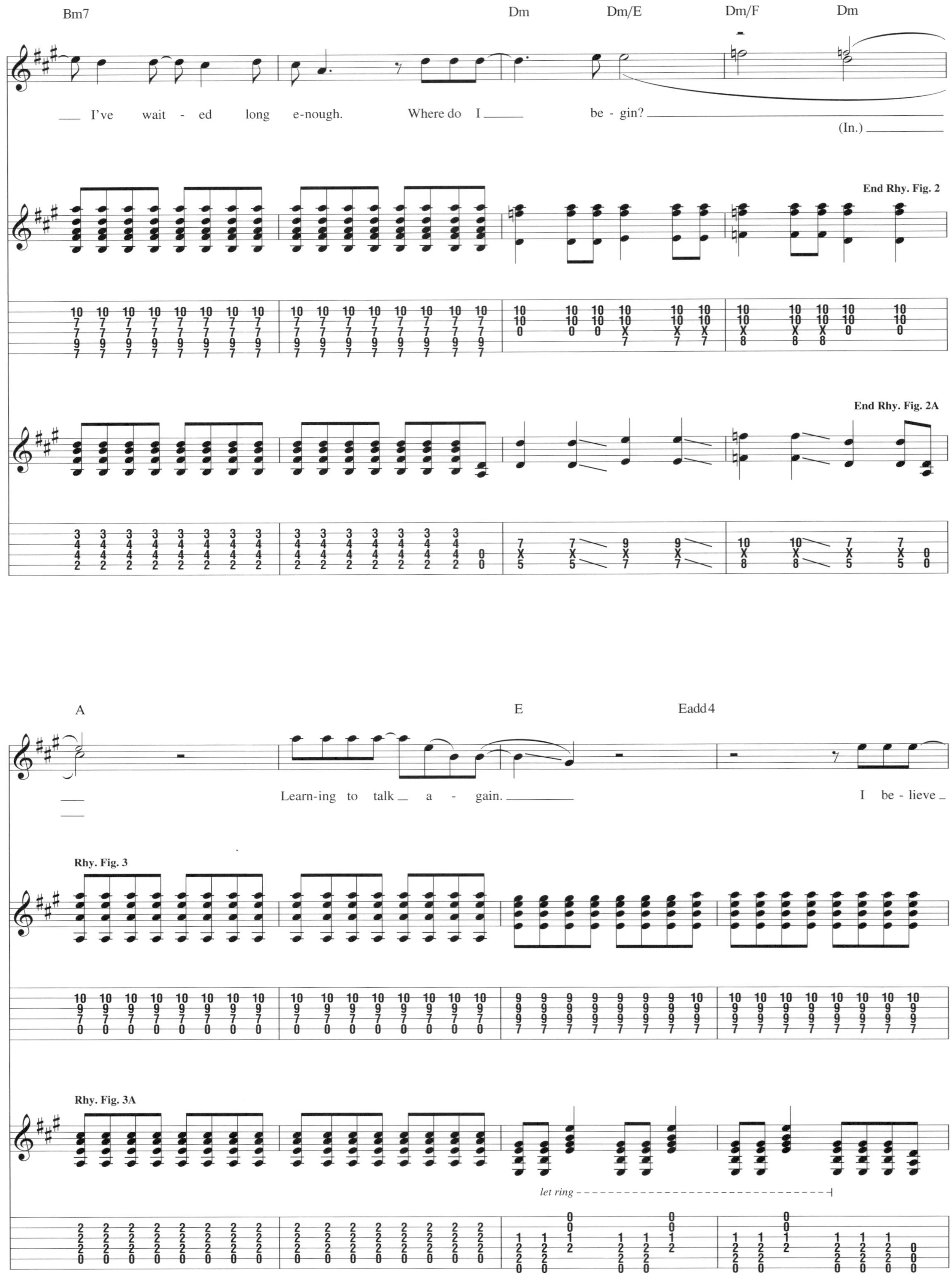

Bm7 | | | Dm | Dm/E | Dm/F | Dm

I've wait-ed long e-nough. Where do I be-gin? (In.)

End Rhy. Fig. 2

End Rhy. Fig. 2A

A | | E | Eadd4

Learn-ing to talk a-gain. I be-lieve

Rhy. Fig. 3

Rhy. Fig. 3A

let ring

Gtr. 4: w/ Riff B (2 times)
E
don't you pay no mind.
Gtr. 1
F#m
D
Dm
End Rhy. Fig. 4A
Set me free again. To
Gtr. 4
Riff C
End Riff C
Gtr. 1
End Rhy. Fig. 4
Gtr. 1: w/ Rhy. Fig. 4 (2 times)
Gtrs. 2 & 3: w/ Rhy. Fig. 4A (2 times)
Gtr. 4: w/ Riff B (5 times)
A
keep alive a moment at a time, but still inside a whisper to a riot. To
E
sacrifice, but knowing to survive. The first to cry another state of mind. I'm

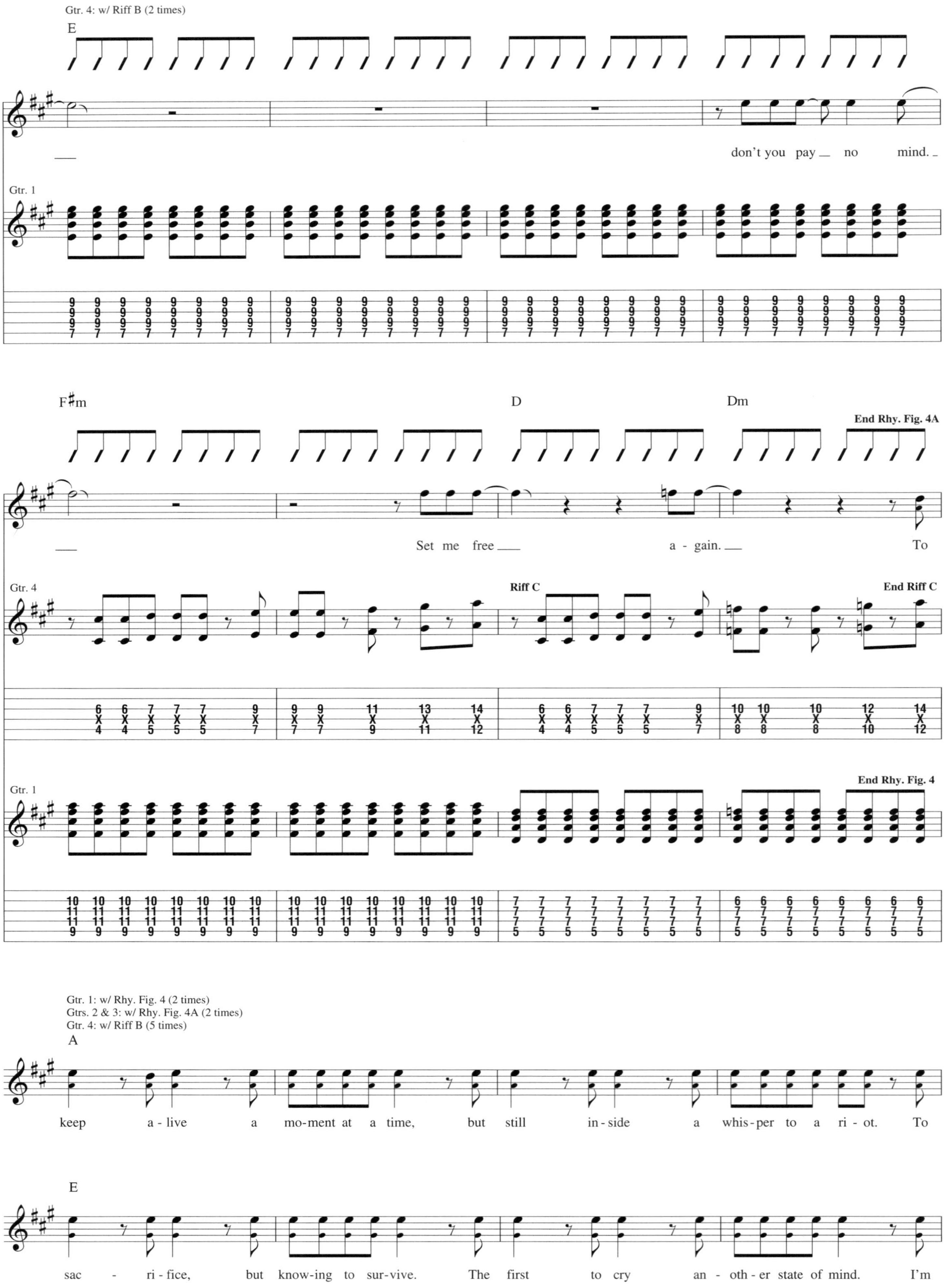

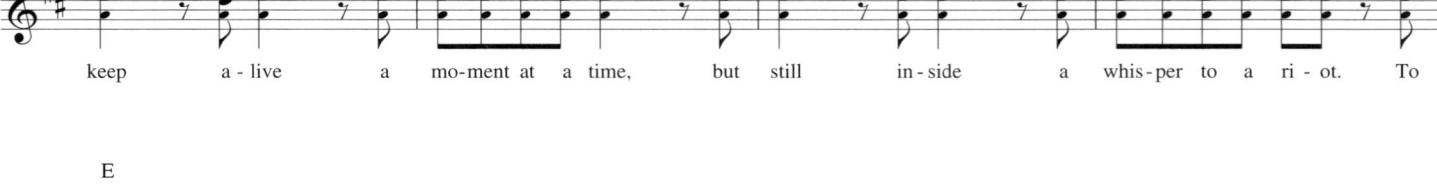

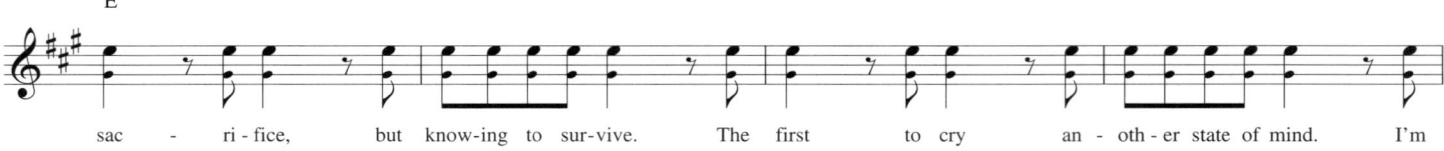

Gtr. 4: w/ Riff C
F♯m
D
Dm
on my knees, I'm pray-ing for a sign. For - ev - er, what-ev - er, I nev - er want to die. I
Gtr. 5 (dist.)
mf
Gtr. 6 (dist.)
mf
Gtr. 4: w/ Riff B (5 times)
A
nev - er want to die. I nev - er want to die. I'm on my knees, I nev - er want to die. I'm

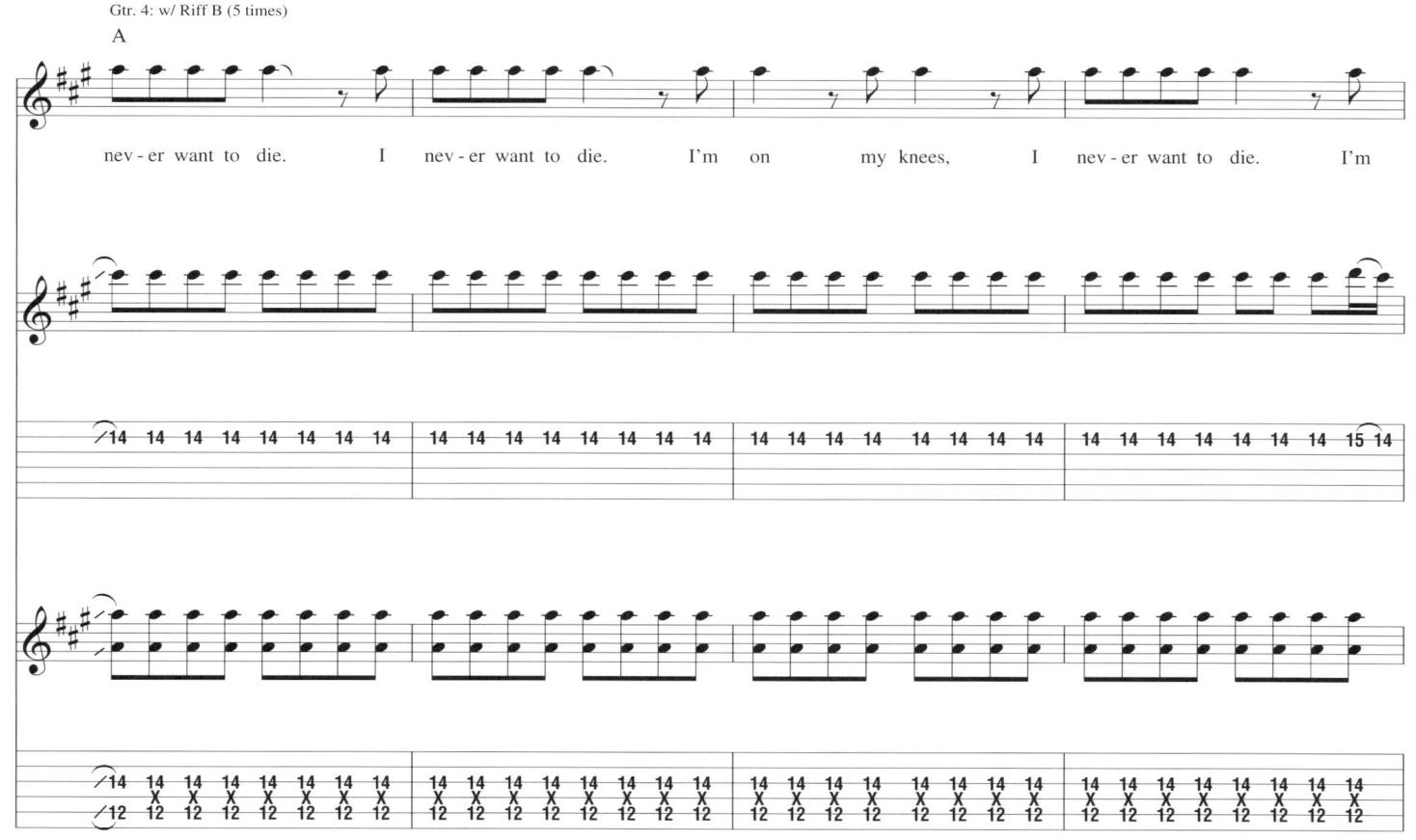

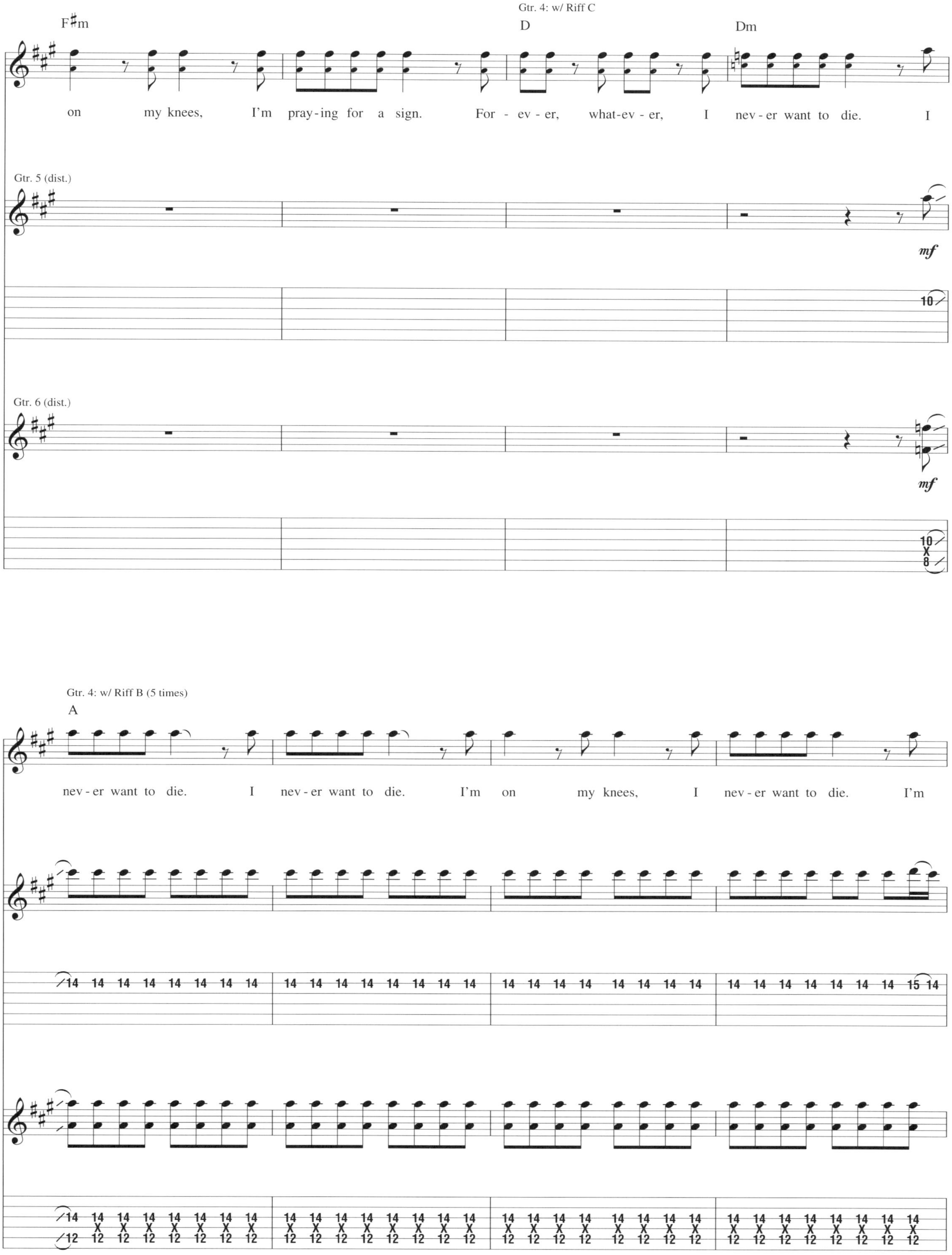

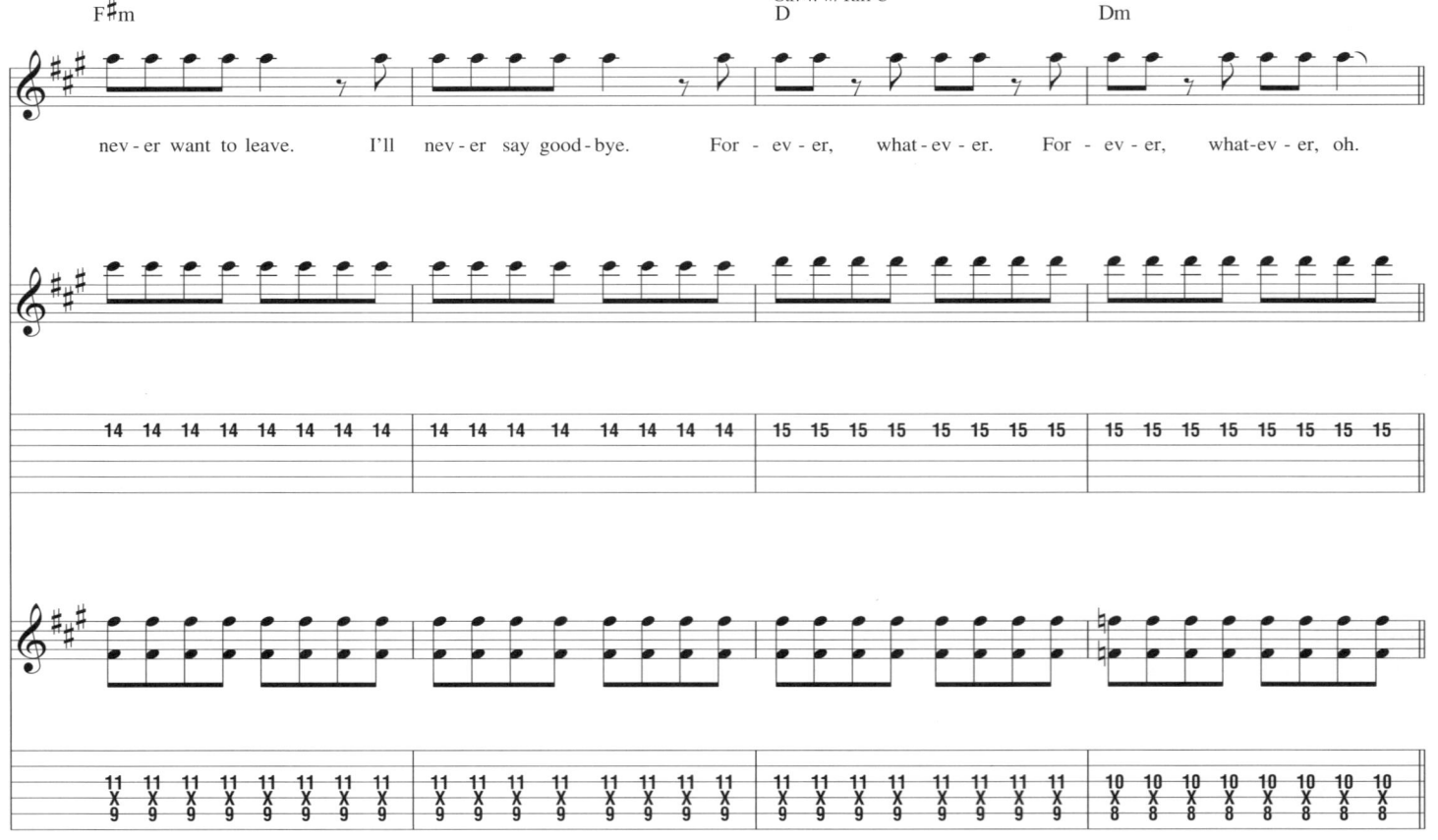

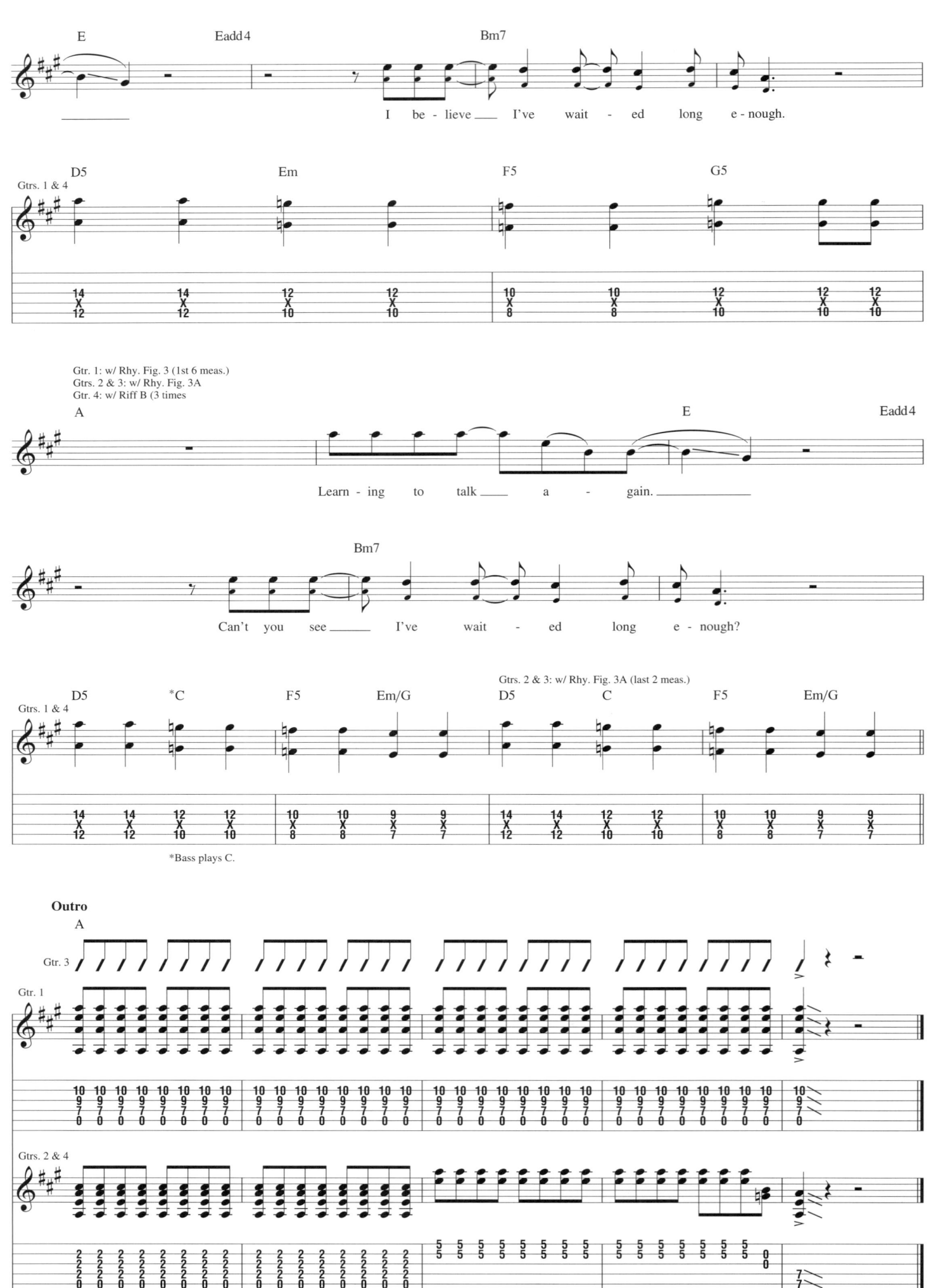

GUITAR NOTATION LEGEND

Guitar music can be notated three different ways: on a *musical staff*, in *tablature*, and in *rhythm slashes*.

RHYTHM SLASHES are written above the staff. Strum chords in the rhythm indicated. Use the chord diagrams found at the top of the first page of the transcription for the appropriate chord voicings. Round noteheads indicate single notes.

THE MUSICAL STAFF shows pitches and rhythms and is divided by bar lines into measures. Pitches are named after the first seven letters of the alphabet.

TABLATURE graphically represents the guitar fingerboard. Each horizontal line represents a string, and each number represents a fret.

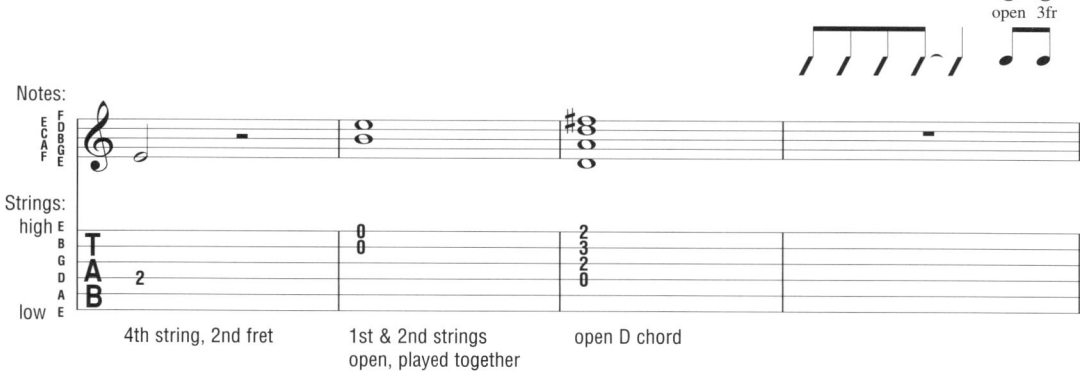

Definitions for Special Guitar Notation

HALF-STEP BEND: Strike the note and bend up 1/2 step.

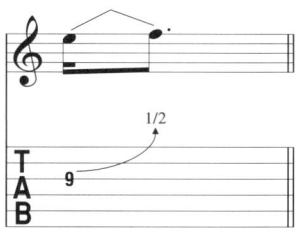

BEND AND RELEASE: Strike the note and bend up as indicated, then release back to the original note. Only the first note is struck.

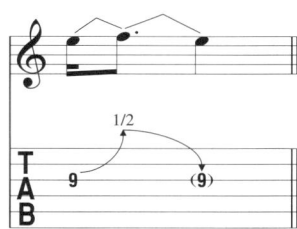

VIBRATO: The string is vibrated by rapidly bending and releasing the note with the fretting hand.

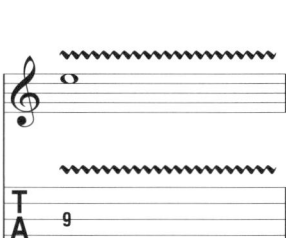

LEGATO SLIDE: Strike the first note and then slide the same fret-hand finger up or down to the second note. The second note is not struck.

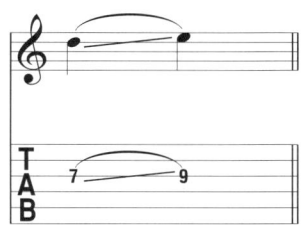

WHOLE-STEP BEND: Strike the note and bend up one step.

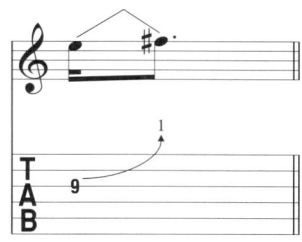

PRE-BEND: Bend the note as indicated, then strike it.

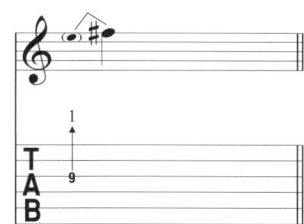

WIDE VIBRATO: The pitch is varied to a greater degree by vibrating with the fretting hand.

SHIFT SLIDE: Same as legato slide, except the second note is struck.

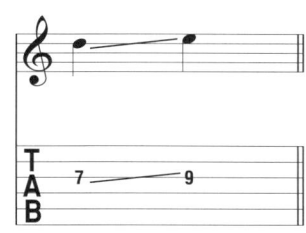

GRACE NOTE BEND: Strike the note and immediately bend up as indicated.

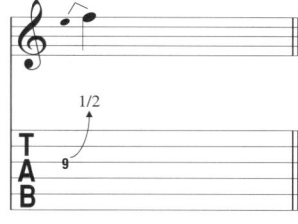

PRE-BEND AND RELEASE: Bend the note as indicated. Strike it and release the bend back to the original note.

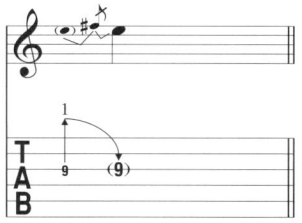

HAMMER-ON: Strike the first (lower) note with one finger, then sound the higher note (on the same string) with another finger by fretting it without picking.

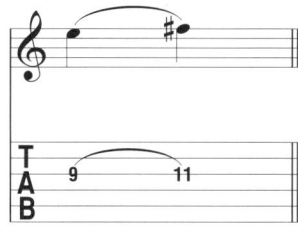

TRILL: Very rapidly alternate between the notes indicated by continuously hammering on and pulling off.

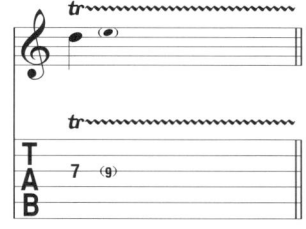

SLIGHT (MICROTONE) BEND: Strike the note and bend up 1/4 step.

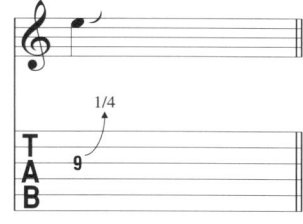

UNISON BEND: Strike the two notes simultaneously and bend the lower note up to the pitch of the higher.

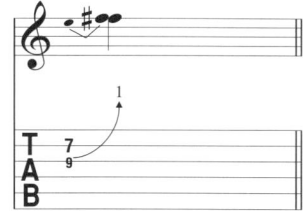

PULL-OFF: Place both fingers on the notes to be sounded. Strike the first note and without picking, pull the finger off to sound the second (lower) note.

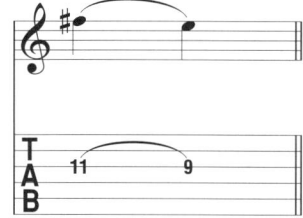

TAPPING: Hammer ("tap") the fret indicated with the pick-hand index or middle finger and pull off to the note fretted by the fret hand.

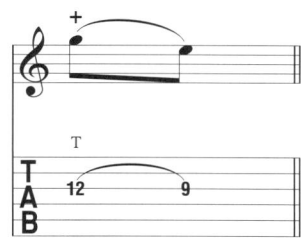

NATURAL HARMONIC: Strike the note while the fret-hand lightly touches the string directly over the fret indicated.

PINCH HARMONIC: The note is fretted normally and a harmonic is produced by adding the edge of the thumb or the tip of the index finger of the pick hand to the normal pick attack.

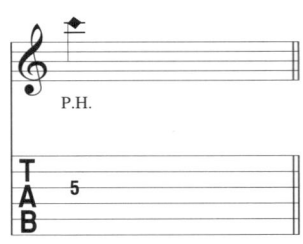

HARP HARMONIC: The note is fretted normally and a harmonic is produced by gently resting the pick hand's index finger directly above the indicated fret (in parentheses) while the pick hand's thumb or pick assists by plucking the appropriate string.

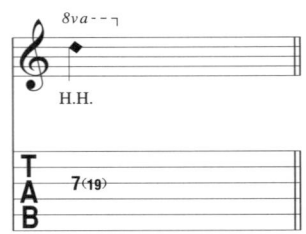

PICK SCRAPE: The edge of the pick is rubbed down (or up) the string, producing a scratchy sound.

MUFFLED STRINGS: A percussive sound is produced by laying the fret hand across the string(s) without depressing, and striking them with the pick hand.

PALM MUTING: The note is partially muted by the pick hand lightly touching the string(s) just before the bridge.

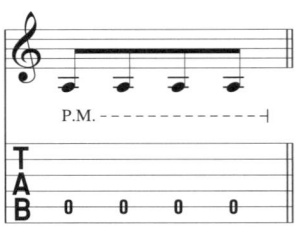

RAKE: Drag the pick across the strings indicated with a single motion.

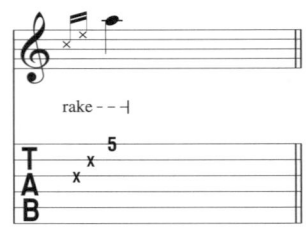

TREMOLO PICKING: The note is picked as rapidly and continuously as possible.

ARPEGGIATE: Play the notes of the chord indicated by quickly rolling them from bottom to top.

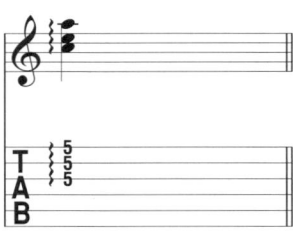

VIBRATO BAR DIVE AND RETURN: The pitch of the note or chord is dropped a specified number of steps (in rhythm), then returned to the original pitch.

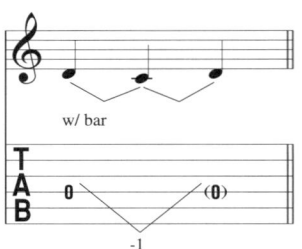

VIBRATO BAR SCOOP: Depress the bar just before striking the note, then quickly release the bar.

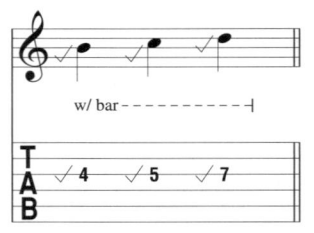

VIBRATO BAR DIP: Strike the note and then immediately drop a specified number of steps, then release back to the original pitch.

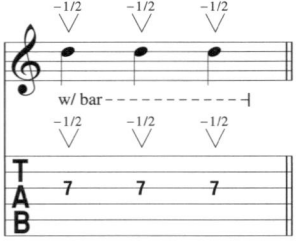

Additional Musical Definitions

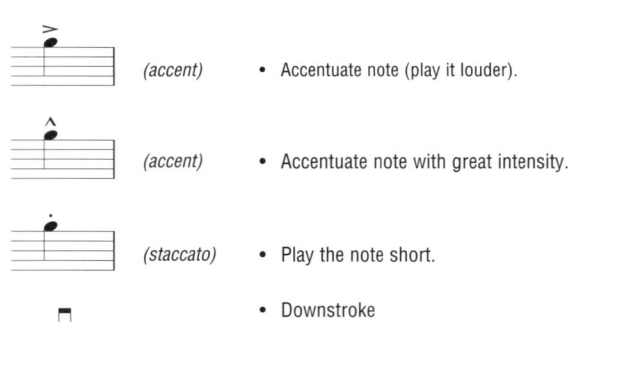

(accent)	• Accentuate note (play it louder).
(accent)	• Accentuate note with great intensity.
(staccato)	• Play the note short.
⊓	• Downstroke
V	• Upstroke
D.S. al Coda	• Go back to the sign (𝄋), then play until the measure marked "*To Coda*," then skip to the section labelled "**Coda**."
D.C. al Fine	• Go back to the beginning of the song and play until the measure marked "*Fine*" (end).

Rhy. Fig.	• Label used to recall a recurring accompaniment pattern (usually chordal).
Riff	• Label used to recall composed, melodic lines (usually single notes) which recur.
Fill	• Label used to identify a brief melodic figure which is to be inserted into the arrangement.
Rhy. Fill	• A chordal version of a Fill.
tacet	• Instrument is silent (drops out).
	• Repeat measures between signs.
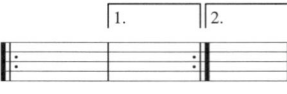	• When a repeated section has different endings, play the first ending only the first time and the second ending only the second time.

NOTE: Tablature numbers in parentheses mean:
1. The note is being sustained over a system (note in standard notation is tied), or
2. The note is sustained, but a new articulation (such as a hammer-on, pull-off, slide or vibrato) begins, or
3. The note is a barely audible "ghost" note (note in standard notation is also in parentheses).

RECORDED VERSIONS
GUITAR®
UTHENTIC TRANSCRIPTIONS
ITH NOTES AND TABLATURE

GUITAR RECORDED VERSIONS®

Guitar Recorded Versions® are note-for-note transcriptions of guitar music taken directly off recordings. This series, one of the most popular in print today, features some of the greatest guitar players and groups from blues and rock to country and jazz.

Guitar Recorded Versions are transcribed by the best transcribers in the business. Every book contains notes and tablature. Visit www.halleonard.com for our complete selection.

041344 The Definitive AC/DC Songbook $39.99
690016 The Will Ackerman Collection $19.95
690501 Bryan Adams – Greatest Hits $19.95
690002 Aerosmith – Big Ones $24.95
692015 Aerosmith – Greatest Hits $22.95
690603 Aerosmith – O Yeah! (Ultimate Hits) $24.95
690147 Aerosmith – Rocks $19.95
690146 Aerosmith – Toys in the Attic $19.99
690139 Alice in Chains $19.95
690178 Alice in Chains – Acoustic $19.95
694865 Alice in Chains – Dirt $19.95
660225 Alice in Chains – Facelift $19.95
694925 Alice in Chains – Jar of Flies/Sap $19.95
690387 Alice in Chains – Nothing Safe: Best of the Box $19.95
690899 All That Remains – The Fall of Ideals $19.95
0691056 All That Remains – For We Are Many $22.99
0690980 All That Remains – Overcome $22.99
0690812 All-American Rejects – Move Along $19.95
0690983 All-American Rejects – When the World Comes Down $22.99
0694932 Allman Brothers Band – Definitive Collection for Guitar Volume 1 $24.95
0694933 Allman Brothers Band – Definitive Collection for Guitar Volume 2 $24.95
0694934 Allman Brothers Band – Definitive Collection for Guitar Volume 3 $24.95
0690958 Duane Allman Guitar Anthology $24.99
0691071 Alter Bridge – AB III $22.99
0690945 Alter Bridge – Blackbird $22.99
0690755 Alter Bridge – One Day Remains $19.95
0690571 Trey Anastasio $19.95
0691013 The Answer – Everyday Demons $19.99
0690158 Chet Atkins – Almost Alone $19.95
0694876 Chet Atkins – Contemporary Styles $19.95
0694878 Chet Atkins – Vintage Fingerstyle $19.95
0690865 Atreyu – A Deathgrip on Yesterday $19.95
0690609 Audioslave $19.95
0690804 Audioslave – Out of Exile $19.95
0690884 Audioslave – Revelations $19.95
0690926 Avenged Sevenfold $22.95
0690820 Avenged Sevenfold – City of Evil $24.95
0694918 Randy Bachman Collection $22.95
0690366 Bad Company – Original Anthology – Book 1 $19.95
0690367 Bad Company – Original Anthology – Book 2 $19.95
690503 Beach Boys – Very Best of $19.95
694929 Beatles: 1962-1966 $24.95
694930 Beatles: 1967-1970 $24.95
690489 Beatles – 1 $24.99
694880 Beatles – Abbey Road $19.95
691066 Beatles – Beatles for Sale $22.99
690110 Beatles – Book 1 (White Album) $19.95
0690111 Beatles – Book 2 (White Album) $19.95
0690902 Beatles – The Capitol Albums, Volume 1 $24.99
0694832 Beatles – For Acoustic Guitar $22.99
0690137 Beatles – A Hard Day's Night $16.95
0691031 Beatles – Help! $19.99
0690482 Beatles – Let It Be $17.95
0691067 Beatles – Meet the Beatles! $22.99
0691068 Beatles – Please Please Me $22.99
0694891 Beatles – Revolver $19.95
0694914 Beatles – Rubber Soul $19.95
0694863 Beatles – Sgt. Pepper's Lonely Hearts Club Band $19.95
0690383 Beatles – Yellow Submarine $19.95
0690632 Beck – Sea Change $19.95
0691041 Jeff Beck – Truth $19.99
0694884 Best of George Benson $19.95
0692385 Chuck Berry $19.95
0690835 Billy Talent $19.95
0690879 Billy Talent II $19.95
0690149 Black Sabbath $14.95
0690901 Best of Black Sabbath $19.95
691010 Black Sabbath – Heaven and Hell $22.99
690148 Black Sabbath – Master of Reality $14.95
690142 Black Sabbath – Paranoid $14.95
692200 Black Sabbath – We Sold Our Soul for Rock 'N' Roll $19.95

00690674 blink-182 $19.95
00690389 blink-182 – Enema of the State $19.95
00690831 blink-182 – Greatest Hits $19.95
00690523 blink-182 – Take Off Your Pants and Jacket $19.95
00690028 Blue Oyster Cult – Cult Classics $19.95
00690851 James Blunt – Back to Bedlam $22.95
00690008 Bon Jovi – Cross Road $19.95
00690913 Boston $19.95
00690932 Boston – Don't Look Back $19.99
00690829 Boston Guitar Collection $19.99
00690491 Best of David Bowie $19.95
00690583 Box Car Racer $19.95
00691023 Breaking Benjamin – Dear Agony $22.99
00690873 Breaking Benjamin – Phobia $19.95
00690764 Breaking Benjamin – We Are Not Alone $19.95
00690451 Jeff Buckley Collection $24.95
00690957 Bullet for My Valentine – Scream Aim Fire $19.95
00690678 Best of Kenny Burrell $19.95
00691077 Cage the Elephant – Thank You, Happy Birthday $22.99
00690564 The Calling – Camino Palmero $19.95
00690261 Carter Family Collection $19.95
00690043 Best of Cheap Trick $19.95
00690171 Chicago – The Definitive Guitar Collection $22.95
00691004 Chickenfoot $22.99
00691011 Chimaira Guitar Collection $24.99
00690567 Charlie Christian – The Definitive Collection $19.95
00690590 Eric Clapton – Anthology $29.95
00692391 Best of Eric Clapton – 2nd Edition $22.95
00691055 Eric Clapton – Clapton $22.99
00690936 Eric Clapton – Complete Clapton $29.99
00690074 Eric Clapton – Cream of Clapton $24.95
00690247 Eric Clapton – 461 Ocean Boulevard $19.99
00690010 Eric Clapton – From the Cradle $19.95
00690716 Eric Clapton – Me and Mr. Johnson $19.95
00694873 Eric Clapton – Timepieces $19.95
00694869 Eric Clapton – Unplugged $22.95
00690415 Clapton Chronicles – Best of Eric Clapton $18.95
00694896 John Mayall/Eric Clapton – Bluesbreakers $19.95
00690162 Best of the Clash $19.95
00690828 Coheed & Cambria – Good Apollo I'm Burning Star, IV, Vol. 1: From Fear Through the Eyes of Madness $19.95
00690940 Coheed and Cambria – No World for Tomorrow $19.95
00690494 Coldplay – Parachutes $19.95
00690593 Coldplay – A Rush of Blood to the Head $19.95
00690906 Coldplay – The Singles & B-Sides $24.95
00690962 Coldplay – Viva La Vida $19.95
00690806 Coldplay – X & Y $19.95
00690855 Best of Collective Soul $19.95
00690928 Chris Cornell – Carry On $19.95
00694940 Counting Crows – August & Everything After $19.95
00690405 Counting Crows – This Desert Life $19.95
00694840 Cream – Disraeli Gears $19.95
00690285 Cream – Those Were the Days $17.95
00690819 Best of Creedence Clearwater Revival $22.95
00690648 The Very Best of Jim Croce $19.95
00690572 Steve Cropper – Soul Man $19.95
00690613 Best of Crosby, Stills & Nash $22.95
00690777 Crossfade $19.95
00699521 The Cure – Greatest Hits $24.95
00690637 Best of Dick Dale $19.95
00690941 Dashboard Confessional – The Shade of Poison Trees $19.95
00690892 Daughtry $19.95
00690822 Best of Alex De Grassi $19.95
00690967 Death Cab for Cutie – Narrow Stairs $22.99
00690289 Best of Deep Purple $17.95
00690288 Deep Purple – Machine Head $17.99
00690784 Best of Def Leppard $19.95
00694831 Derek and the Dominos – Layla & Other Assorted Love Songs $22.95
00692240 Bo Diddley – Guitar Solos by Fred Sokolow $19.99
00690384 Best of Ani DiFranco $19.95
00690322 Ani DiFranco – Little Plastic Castle $19.95
00690380 Ani DiFranco – Up Up Up Up Up Up $19.95
00690979 Best of Dinosaur Jr. $19.99

00690833 Private Investigations – Best of Dire Straits and Mark Knopfler $24.95
00695382 Very Best of Dire Straits – Sultans of Swing $22.95
00690347 The Doors – Anthology $22.95
00690348 The Doors – Essential Guitar Collection $16.95
00690915 Dragonforce – Inhuman Rampage $29.99
00690250 Best of Duane Eddy $16.95
00690533 Electric Light Orchestra Guitar Collection $19.95
00690909 Best of Tommy Emmanuel $19.95
00690555 Best of Melissa Etheridge $19.95
00690496 Best of Everclear $19.95
00690515 Extreme II – Pornograffitti $19.95
00690982 Fall Out Boy – Folie à Deux $22.99
00690810 Fall Out Boy – From Under the Cork Tree $19.95
00691009 Five Finger Death Punch $19.99
00690664 Best of Fleetwood Mac $19.95
00690870 Flyleaf $19.95
00690257 John Fogerty – Blue Moon Swamp $19.95
00690931 Foo Fighters – Echoes, Silence, Patience & Grace $19.95
00690808 Foo Fighters – In Your Honor $19.95
00690805 Best of Robben Ford $19.95
00690842 Best of Peter Frampton $19.95
00690734 Franz Ferdinand $19.95
00694920 Best of Free $19.95
00694807 Danny Gatton – 88 Elmira St $19.95
00690438 Genesis Guitar Anthology $19.95
00690753 Best of Godsmack $19.95
00120167 Godsmack $19.95
00690848 Godsmack – IV $19.95
00690338 Goo Goo Dolls – Dizzy Up the Girl $19.95
00690576 Goo Goo Dolls – Gutterflower $19.95
00690927 Patty Griffin – Children Running Through $19.95
00690591 Patty Griffin – Guitar Collection $19.95
00690978 Guns N' Roses – Chinese Democracy $24.99
00691027 Buddy Guy Anthology $24.99
00694854 Buddy Guy – Damn Right, I've Got the Blues $19.95
00690697 Best of Jim Hall $19.95
00690840 Ben Harper – Both Sides of the Gun $19.95
00690987 Ben Harper and Relentless7 – White Lies for Dark Times $22.99
00694798 George Harrison Anthology $19.95
00690778 Hawk Nelson – Letters to the President $19.95
00690841 Scott Henderson – Blues Guitar Collection $19.95
00692930 Jimi Hendrix – Are You Experienced? $24.95
00692931 Jimi Hendrix – Axis: Bold As Love $22.95
00690304 Jimi Hendrix – Band of Gypsys $24.99
00690321 Jimi Hendrix – BBC Sessions $22.95
00690608 Jimi Hendrix – Blue Wild Angel $24.95
00694944 Jimi Hendrix – Blues $24.95
00692932 Jimi Hendrix – Electric Ladyland $24.95
00690602 Jimi Hendrix – Smash Hits $24.99
00691033 Jimi Hendrix – Valleys of Neptune $22.99
00690017 Jimi Hendrix – Woodstock $24.95
00690843 H.I.M. – Dark Light $19.95
00690869 Hinder – Extreme Behavior $19.95
00660029 Buddy Holly $19.95
00690793 John Lee Hooker Anthology $24.99
00660169 John Lee Hooker – A Blues Legend $19.95
00694905 Howlin' Wolf $19.95
00690692 Very Best of Billy Idol $19.95
00690688 Incubus – A Crow Left of the Murder $19.95
00690544 Incubus – Morningview $19.95
00690136 Indigo Girls – 1200 Curfews $22.95
00690790 Iron Maiden Anthology $24.99
00691058 Iron Maiden – The Final Frontier $22.99
00690887 Iron Maiden – A Matter of Life and Death $24.95
00690730 Alan Jackson – Guitar Collection $19.95
00694938 Elmore James – Master Electric Slide Guitar $19.95
00690652 Best of Jane's Addiction $19.95
00690721 Jet – Get Born $19.95
00690684 Jethro Tull – Aqualung $19.95
00690693 Jethro Tull Guitar Anthology $19.95
00690647 Best of Jewel $19.95
00690898 John 5 – The Devil Knows My Name $22.95
00690959 John 5 – Requiem $22.95

Code	Title	Price
00690814	John 5 – Songs for Sanity	$19.95
00690751	John 5 – Vertigo	$19.95
00694912	Eric Johnson – Ah Via Musicom	$19.95
00690660	Best of Eric Johnson	$19.95
00690845	Eric Johnson – Bloom	$19.95
00690169	Eric Johnson – Venus Isle	$22.95
00690846	Jack Johnson and Friends – Sing-A-Longs and Lullabies for the Film Curious George	$19.95
00690271	Robert Johnson – The New Transcriptions	$24.95
00699131	Best of Janis Joplin	$19.95
00690427	Best of Judas Priest	$22.99
00690651	Juanes – Exitos de Juanes	$19.95
00690277	Best of Kansas	$19.95
00690911	Best of Phil Keaggy	$24.99
00690727	Toby Keith Guitar Collection	$19.95
00690742	The Killers – Hot Fuss	$19.95
00690888	The Killers – Sam's Town	$19.95
00690504	Very Best of Albert King	$19.95
00690444	B.B. King & Eric Clapton – Riding with the King	$19.95
00690134	Freddie King Collection	$19.95
00691062	Kings of Leon – Come Around Sundown	$22.99
00690975	Kings of Leon – Only by the Night	$22.99
00690339	Best of the Kinks	$19.95
00690157	Kiss – Alive!	$19.95
00690356	Kiss – Alive II	$22.99
00694903	Best of Kiss for Guitar	$24.95
00690355	Kiss – Destroyer	$16.95
14026320	Mark Knopfler – Get Lucky	$22.99
00690164	Mark Knopfler Guitar – Vol. 1	$19.95
00690163	Mark Knopfler/Chet Atkins – Neck and Neck	$19.95
00690780	Korn – Greatest Hits, Volume 1	$22.95
00690836	Korn – See You on the Other Side	$19.95
00690377	Kris Kristofferson Collection	$19.95
00690861	Kutless – Hearts of the Innocent	$19.95
00690834	Lamb of God – Ashes of the Wake	$19.95
00690875	Lamb of God – Sacrament	$19.95
00690977	Ray LaMontagne – Gossip in the Grain	$19.99
00690890	Ray LaMontagne – Till the Sun Turns Black	$19.95
00690823	Ray LaMontagne – Trouble	$19.95
00691057	Ray LaMontagne and the Pariah Dogs – God Willin' & The Creek Don't Rise	$22.99
00690658	Johnny Lang – Long Time Coming	$19.95
00690726	Avril Lavigne – Under My Skin	$19.95
00690679	John Lennon – Guitar Collection	$19.95
00690781	Linkin Park – Hybrid Theory	$22.95
00690782	Linkin Park – Meteora	$22.95
00690922	Linkin Park – Minutes to Midnight	$19.95
00690783	Best of Live	$19.95
00699623	The Best of Chuck Loeb	$19.95
00690743	Los Lonely Boys	$19.95
00690720	Lostprophets – Start Something	$19.95
00690525	Best of George Lynch	$24.99
00690955	Lynyrd Skynyrd – All-Time Greatest Hits	$19.99
00694954	New Best of Lynyrd Skynyrd	$19.95
00690577	Yngwie Malmsteen – Anthology	$24.95
00694845	Yngwie Malmsteen – Fire and Ice	$19.95
00694755	Yngwie Malmsteen's Rising Force	$19.95
00694757	Yngwie Malmsteen – Trilogy	$19.95
00690754	Marilyn Manson – Lest We Forget	$19.95
00694956	Bob Marley – Legend	$19.95
00690548	Very Best of Bob Marley & The Wailers – One Love	$22.99
00694945	Bob Marley – Songs of Freedom	$24.95
00690914	Maroon 5 – It Won't Be Soon Before Long	$19.95
00690657	Maroon 5 – Songs About Jane	$19.95
00690748	Maroon 5 – 1.22.03 Acoustic	$19.95
00690989	Mastodon – Crack the Skye	$22.99
00690442	Matchbox 20 – Mad Season	$19.95
00690616	Matchbox Twenty – More Than You Think You Are	$19.95
00690239	Matchbox 20 – Yourself or Someone like You	$19.95
00691034	Andy McKee – Joyland	$19.99
00690382	Sarah McLachlan – Mirrorball	$19.95
00120080	The Don McLean Songbook	$19.95
00694952	Megadeth – Countdown to Extinction	$22.95
00690244	Megadeth – Cryptic Writings	$19.95
00694951	Megadeth – Rust in Peace	$22.95
00690011	Megadeth – Youthanasia	$19.95
00690505	John Mellencamp Guitar Collection	$19.95
00690562	Pat Metheny – Bright Size Life	$19.95
00690646	Pat Metheny – One Quiet Night	$19.95
00690559	Pat Metheny – Question & Answer	$19.95
00690040	Steve Miller Band Greatest Hits	$19.95
00690769	Modest Mouse – Good News for People Who Love Bad News	$19.95
00694802	Gary Moore – Still Got the Blues	$22.95
00691005	Best of Motion City Soundtrack	$19.95
00690787	Mudvayne – L.D. 50	$22.95
00690996	My Morning Jacket Collection	$19.99
00690984	Matt Nathanson – Some Mad Hope	$22.99
00690611	Nirvana	$22.95
00694895	Nirvana – Bleach	$19.95
00690189	Nirvana – From the Muddy Banks of the Wishkah	$19.95
00694913	Nirvana – In Utero	$19.95
00694883	Nirvana – Nevermind	$19.95
00690026	Nirvana – Unplugged in New York	$19.95
00120112	No Doubt – Tragic Kingdom	$22.95
00690121	Oasis – (What's the Story) Morning Glory	$19.95
00690226	Oasis – The Other Side of Oasis	$19.95
00690358	The Offspring – Americana	$19.95
00690203	The Offspring – Smash	$18.95
00690818	The Best of Opeth	$22.95
00691052	Roy Orbison – Black & White Night	$22.95
00694847	Best of Ozzy Osbourne	$22.95
00690921	Ozzy Osbourne – Black Rain	$19.95
00690399	Ozzy Osbourne – The Ozzman Cometh	$19.95
00690129	Ozzy Osbourne – Ozzmosis	$22.95
00690933	Best of Brad Paisley	$22.95
00690995	Brad Paisley – Play: The Guitar Album	$24.99
00690866	Panic! At the Disco – A Fever You Can't Sweat Out	$19.95
00690885	Papa Roach – The Paramour Sessions	$19.95
00690939	Christopher Parkening – Solo Pieces	$19.99
00690594	Best of Les Paul	$19.95
00694855	Pearl Jam – Ten	$19.95
00690439	A Perfect Circle – Mer De Noms	$19.95
00690661	A Perfect Circle – Thirteenth Step	$19.95
00690725	Best of Carl Perkins	$19.99
00690499	Tom Petty – Definitive Guitar Collection	$19.95
00698868	Tom Petty – Highway Companion	$19.95
00690176	Phish – Billy Breathes	$22.95
00690428	Pink Floyd – Dark Side of the Moon	$19.95
00690789	Best of Poison	$19.95
00693864	Best of The Police	$19.95
00690299	Best of Elvis: The King of Rock 'n' Roll	$19.95
00692535	Elvis Presley	$19.95
00690003	Classic Queen	$24.95
00694975	Queen – Greatest Hits	$24.95
00690670	Very Best of Queensryche	$19.95
00690878	The Raconteurs – Broken Boy Soldiers	$19.95
00694910	Rage Against the Machine	$19.95
00690179	Rancid – And Out Come the Wolves	$22.95
00690426	Best of Ratt	$19.95
00690055	Red Hot Chili Peppers – Blood Sugar Sex Magik	$19.95
00690584	Red Hot Chili Peppers – By the Way	$19.95
00690379	Red Hot Chili Peppers – Californication	$19.95
00690673	Red Hot Chili Peppers – Greatest Hits	$19.95
00690090	Red Hot Chili Peppers – One Hot Minute	$22.95
00690852	Red Hot Chili Peppers – Stadium Arcadium	$24.95
00690893	The Red Jumpsuit Apparatus – Don't You Fake It	$19.95
00690511	Django Reinhardt – The Definitive Collection	$19.95
00690779	Relient K – MMHMM	$19.95
00690643	Relient K – Two Lefts Don't Make a Right ... But Three Do	$19.95
00694899	R.E.M. – Automatic for the People	$19.95
00690260	Jimmie Rodgers Guitar Collection	$19.95
00690014	Rolling Stones – Exile on Main Street	$24.95
00690631	Rolling Stones – Guitar Anthology	$27.95
00690685	David Lee Roth – Eat 'Em and Smile	$19.95
00690031	Santana's Greatest Hits	$19.95
00690796	Very Best of Michael Schenker	$19.95
00690566	Best of Scorpions	$22.95
00690604	Bob Seger – Guitar Anthology	$19.95
00690659	Bob Seger and the Silver Bullet Band – Greatest Hits, Volume 2	$17.95
00691012	Shadows Fall – Retribution	$22.99
00690896	Shadows Fall – Threads of Life	$19.95
00690803	Best of Kenny Wayne Shepherd Band	$19.95
00690750	Kenny Wayne Shepherd – The Place You're In	$19.95
00690857	Shinedown – Us and Them	$19.95
00690196	Silverchair – Freak Show	$19.95
00690130	Silverchair – Frogstomp	$19.95
00690872	Slayer – Christ Illusion	$19.95
00690813	Slayer – Guitar Collection	$19.95
00690419	Slipknot	$19.95
00690973	Slipknot – All Hope Is Gone	$22.99
00690733	Slipknot – Volume 3 (The Subliminal Verses)	$22.99
00690330	Social Distortion – Live at the Roxy	$19.95
00120004	Best of Steely Dan	$24.95
00694921	Best of Steppenwolf	$22.95
00690655	Best of Mike Stern	$19.95
00690949	Rod Stewart Guitar Anthology	$19.99
00690021	Sting – Fields of Gold	$19.95
00690597	Stone Sour	$19.95
00690689	Story of the Year – Page Avenue	$19.95
00690520	Styx Guitar Collection	$19.95
00120081	Sublime	$19.95

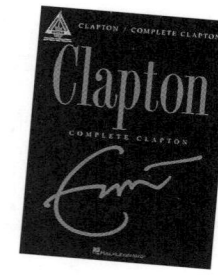

Code	Title	Price
00690992	Sublime – Robbin' the Hood	$19.99
00690519	SUM 41 – All Killer No Filler	$19.95
00690994	Taylor Swift	$22.99
00690993	Taylor Swift – Fearless	$22.99
00691063	Taylor Swift – Speak Now	$22.99
00690767	Switchfoot – The Beautiful Letdown	$19.95
00690425	System of a Down	$19.95
00690830	System of a Down – Hypnotize	$19.95
00690799	System of a Down – Mezmerize	$19.95
00690531	System of a Down – Toxicity	$19.95
00690824	Best of James Taylor	$16.95
00694887	Best of Thin Lizzy	$19.95
00690671	Three Days Grace	$19.95
00690871	Three Days Grace – One-X	$19.95
00690737	3 Doors Down – The Better Life	$22.95
00690891	30 Seconds to Mars – A Beautiful Lie	$19.95
00690030	Toad the Wet Sprocket	$19.95
00690654	Best of Train	$19.95
00690233	The Merle Travis Collection	$19.99
00690683	Robin Trower – Bridge of Sighs	$19.95
00699191	U2 – Best of: 1980-1990	$19.95
00690732	U2 – Best of: 1990-2000	$19.95
00690894	U2 – 18 Singles	$19.95
00690775	U2 – How to Dismantle an Atomic Bomb	$22.95
00690997	U2 – No Line on the Horizon	$19.99
00690039	Steve Vai – Alien Love Secrets	$24.95
00690172	Steve Vai – Fire Garden	$24.95
00660137	Steve Vai – Passion & Warfare	$24.95
00690881	Steve Vai – Real Illusions: Reflections	$24.95
00694904	Steve Vai – Sex and Religion	$24.95
00690392	Steve Vai – The Ultra Zone	$19.95
00690024	Stevie Ray Vaughan – Couldn't Stand the Weather	$19.95
00690370	Stevie Ray Vaughan and Double Trouble – The Real Deal: Greatest Hits Volume 2	$22.95
00690116	Stevie Ray Vaughan – Guitar Collection	$24.95
00660136	Stevie Ray Vaughan – In Step	$19.95
00694879	Stevie Ray Vaughan – In the Beginning	$19.95
00660058	Stevie Ray Vaughan – Lightnin' Blues '83-'87	$24.95
00690036	Stevie Ray Vaughan – Live Alive	$24.95
00694835	Stevie Ray Vaughan – The Sky Is Crying	$22.95
00690025	Stevie Ray Vaughan – Soul to Soul	$19.95
00690015	Stevie Ray Vaughan – Texas Flood	$19.95
00690772	Velvet Revolver – Contraband	$22.95
00690132	The T-Bone Walker Collection	$19.95
00694789	Muddy Waters – Deep Blues	$24.95
00690071	Weezer (The Blue Album)	$19.95
00690516	Weezer (The Green Album)	$19.95
00690286	Weezer – Pinkerton	$19.95
00691046	Weezer – Rarities Edition	$22.99
00690447	Best of the Who	$24.95
00694970	The Who – Definitive Guitar Collection: A-E	$24.95
00694971	The Who – Definitive Guitar Collection F-Li	$24.95
00694972	The Who – Definitive Guitar Collection: Lo-R	$24.95
00694973	The Who – Definitive Guitar Collection: S-Y	$24.95
00690672	Best of Dar Williams	$19.95
00691017	Wolfmother – Cosmic Egg	$22.99
00690319	Stevie Wonder – Some of the Best	$17.95
00690596	Best of the Yardbirds	$19.95
00690844	Yellowcard – Lights and Sounds	$19.95
00690916	The Best of Dwight Yoakam	$19.95
00690904	Neil Young – Harvest	$24.99
00690905	Neil Young – Rust Never Sleeps	$19.99
00690443	Frank Zappa – Hot Rats	$19.95
00690623	Frank Zappa – Over-Nite Sensation	$22.99
00690589	ZZ Top – Guitar Anthology	$24.95
00690960	ZZ Top Guitar Classics	$19.99

FOR MORE INFORMATION, SEE YOUR LOCAL MUSIC DEALER, OR WRITE TO:

7777 W. BLUEMOUND RD. P.O. BOX 13819 MILWAUKEE, WI 53213

Complete songlists and more at www.halleonard.com
Prices, contents, and availability subject to change without notice.

0611